More Board Games

Desi Scarpone

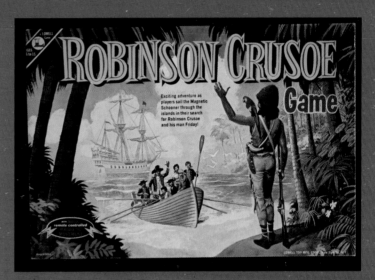

Schiffer Publishing Ltd

4880 Lower Valley Road, Atglen, PA 19310 USA

Disclaimer

The prices listed for games in this book are estimates based on the author's personal experience. They are formatted from a variety of sources including swap meets, game lists, auction catalogs, toy shows, collectible conventions, and the Internet. There are many different factors that contribute to a Seller's asking price but only one factor that determines what a game is worth: what the Buyer is willing to pay. With that in mind, neither the author nor the publisher can be held responsible for any fiscal losses that occur through the use of this book in the purchase or sale of games.

Copyright © 2000 by Desi Scarpone
Library of Congress Card Number: 00-101289

Designed by "Sue"
Type set in Van Dijk/Humanist 521 BT

ISBN: 0-7643-1161-1
Printed in China
1 2 3 4

For More Information on Board Games

You can check out these Internet web sites...

GAMES GONE BY (my web page) Http://www.Gamesgoneby.homepage.com
SID SACKSON WEBPAGE Http://www.webnoir.com/bob/sackson.htm
THE GAME SHOW HOME GAME HOME PAGE Http://www.userdata.acd.net/ ottinger/games.htm
JEFF LOWE'S ExtravaGAMEza Http://www.ewtech.com/games

Published by Schiffer Publishing Ltd.
4880 Lower Valley Road
Atglen, PA 19310
Phone: (610) 593-1777; Fax: (610) 593-2002
E-mail: Schifferbk@aol.com
Please visit our web site catalog at **www.schifferbooks.com**
We are always looking for people to write books on new and related subjects. If you have an idea for a book please contact us at the above address.

This book may be purchased from the publisher.
Include $3.95 for shipping.
Please try your bookstore first.
You may write for a free catalog.

In Europe, Schiffer books are distributed by
Bushwood Books
6 Marksbury Ave.
Kew Gardens
Surrey TW9 4JF England
Phone: 44 (0)208 392-8585
Fax: 44 (0)208 392-9876
E-mail: Bushwd@aol.com
Free postage in the UK. Europe: air mail at cost

Acknowledgments

I would like to thank the many wonderful people who have shared their insights, and their game collections, in the preparation of this book:

Peter Schiffer, for finding a way to make the second book happen. Tom Fassbender, of Uglytown Productions, for unraveling the mystery of Milton Bradley's THE ICE CUBE GAME. To Michael Quinn, who shared his thoughts ... and some of his games for the REMCO INDUSTRIES section. Thanks go to Bob Claster, who allowed me into his home to photograph his huge, though precarious, board game collection, and who shared his thoughts and views. Bob has created a website on the internet that is a tribute to Sid Sackson, one of the premier game creators of all time. The site can be viewed at Http://www.webnoir.com/bob/sackson.htm and is definitely worth a look. Thanks also go to Matt Ottinger, who was able to share many scarce game show board games from his personal collection, despite his arduous schedule. Matt also runs the best, and most complete, website on the subject of game show games in the world, entitled "THE GAME SHOW HOME GAME HOME PAGE". You can view it at Http://www.userdata.acd.net/ottinger/games.htm. Believe me, ANYTHING you want to know about game show games can be found at Matt's entertaining site. I am indebted to Jeff Lowe for taking the time to share more of his incredible collection, for the second time. Jeff is also an excellent source for those collectors looking to purchase board games. His website, Jeff Lowe's ExtravaGAMEza, can be viewed at Http://www.ewtech.com/games. You can also Email him at Gamesguy1@aol.com or call him at (402) 592-8186. If he doesn't have what you're looking for in his huge inventory, he will find it for you. Special thanks are due for Rick Polizzi who, like Jeff, contributed greatly to my first book and now this one. Rick shared his expertise and opinions (each of which he has in abundance), and again allowed me unlimited access to his beautifully displayed collection. Many of the rare games in this book are his. Rick is the author of SPIN AGAIN (published by Chronicle Books 1991), and BABY BOOMER GAMES (published by Collector Books 1995), two fabulous books which no serious collector of board games should be without. You can write to him for back issues of his excellent game-related enterprise SPIN AGAIN MAGAZINE at his email address: Spinagain7@aol.com.

To all who have contributed to this book ... my thanks.

Contents

Introduction   4

Determining Values   5

Chapter One. Western and Military Games   6

Chapter Two. Business, Bookshelf, and Sports Games   17

Chapter Three. Remco Industries   38

Chapter Four. General Games   49

Chapter Five. Entertainment Games   123

Index   175

Introduction

Since the publication of my first book, I have heard from many people. Some of them are looking for games, others just want to share their experiences with board games while growing up. But among these letters, a common theme has developed: many find the board games of today lacking in some respects. I hear from countless parents who want their children to experience the same joy they did while growing up, so they go to their local toy store and buy their kids a game like CANDYLAND. "But," they lament, "it's not the same, even though it plays the same. It's ... different somehow." What is the missing ingredient? I believe it's the artwork. Half of our experience comes from the innocent, often beautiful art that adorns the covers of so many board games. The original cover art to CANDYLAND, with it's quaintly dressed children not quite sure what to make of the talking gingerbread man and his candy house, is comforting and reassuring. It reminds us of a time and place when things were simpler, and the artwork reflects it. The sheer happiness on the plastic face of SPUDSIE, THE HOT POTATO assures us of a smile no matter how we're feeling, while ANY of the covers of early Cadaco-Ellis games, like RED HERRING or OLD MOTHER HUBBARD, are sure to delight and amuse us. Some games, like RANGER RICK AND THE GREAT FOREST FIRE have a cover that can only be described as breathtaking. Game play is important too; but, you're much more likely to buy a bad game with a good cover than a good game with a bad cover.

Many games today utilize photo covers, mainly because it is often cheaper than hiring an artist to paint a cover. The result is often stark and unappealing. Board games are a form of escapist entertainment, and having the contents presented unadorned often results in the game not being shown to its best advantage. Not that game makers have to lie (after all, there are Truth in Advertising laws), but a little fantasy doesn't hurt. There are splendid painted covers nowadays, and many of them DO hark back to a drawing style reminiscent of vintage board games (what does THAT say?), but the majority are unimaginative renderings that do little to make the consumer feel comfortable, reassured, or happy. Having said this, it is entirely possible that the children of the 1990s, like all generations before them, will become nostalgic for the games of their youth.

In the end, games stay with us. They have been amusing, delighting, and, yes, inspiring us for over 150 years. We grow up with games, we learn from games, we teach with games. They touch us on a deep emotional level that we do not often realize, like so many things, until we no longer have them. Board games have given us a lot, and we respond to that gift by cherishing and treasuring them as much as we can.

Using This Book

More Board Games is an excellent reference guide for the veteran collector, eager neophyte, or curious newcomer. Over one thousand different games are shown (many in detail). The wide range of subject matter covered is certain to inform, entertain, and delight the reader.

In addition, *Board Games*, my first book by Schiffer Publishing, is a splendid companion to this volume. It also has over one thousand photos. The chapter headings in this volume correspond to those in that previous work. In some instances, you will see references in this book to items from that text, since there are many relationships to games from that initial foray.

Together, these two books make formidable tools. Individually, each books stands alone well, with valuable information for the beginning, intermediate, and advanced collector alike.

Determining values

The value of board games has become increasingly arbitrary. Condition, rarity, location, cover art, and current market trends should be considered when buying or selling, but sometimes emotion is the only criteria. Separating your feelings from the deal is difficult, but it may save you money, whether you are the buyer or the seller.

The value ranges given in this book are for games that are from Very Good to Very Fine condition, meaning games ranging from those that may be missing a part or two—and have been used (but not abused), to games that are absolutely complete and look as if they have hardly been played with. Games that are still sealed in their original plastic wrapping are usually worth much more than stated, and games that look like they've been through a wringer and are missing essential pieces are worth far less.

Prices for Collectibles in general, and Board Games specifically, have been affected by a growing phenomenon: The Internet. Whether you love it or hate it, there can be no denying the impact it has made. The question is, how do you realistically measure an item's intrinsic value when so many new variables have been introduced. Not only have many more common and obscure games been brought to light, but the sheer numbers of collectors (and non-collectors) desiring them has grown tremendously, fueled in part because of another resurgence of interest in Baby Boomer Collectibles, and in part by ease of access.

EVERYONE has access to a computer, and can log on to a myriad of Web Sites that buy, sell or auction board games.

With this giant wave of humanity sweeping cyberspace, it has become increasingly difficult to determine what might be a legitimate new value, or what is simply spur-of-the-moment "internet" fever. For example, on one auction website, I witnessed the MASH TRIVIA GAME going for $135, while a few inches down the screen, an identical game was going for $5. Someone probably desperately needed the game for a gift of some kind, and—apparently without taking the time to check out similar listings—decided money was no object. This does not a new value make! However, some games, like Milton Bradley's MYSTERY DATE and DARK TOWER, have consistently been selling for hundreds of dollars. There seems to be no letup in the demand for these games, although they are by no means rare.

I still don't feel these prices are "real" (based on my experience); but, they have been realized enough times to say "this is now what this item is worth," for the present moment. The Internet is still in its infancy, and whole new sets of challenges to board game values are sure to emerge in the future.

Finding a pattern, a consistency in sales, is the key to separating the highs from the lows. Also remember that a price guide is just that: a "guide."

Chapter One
Western and Military Games

Who hasn't wanted to be a cowboy at some point while growing up? Games about the West were sporadic until the wide spread introduction of television in the 1950s, and then the floodgates opened. Personalities from Annie Oakley to Jesse James were immortalized in board games through the years, and but a small sample is represented here.

Military games have always been predominantly strategy games, whether commemorating or emulating wars and conflicts through-

out history. Although in today's world it is considered anathema to glorify war, times used to be different. Games that taught about or reenacted famous campaigns were quite popular, and many a company's bread and butter. Games such as Toy Creations' 1942 SPOT-A-PLANE even provided a public service (they felt), helping players identify friendly and enemy aircraft in the event of an attack on American soil.

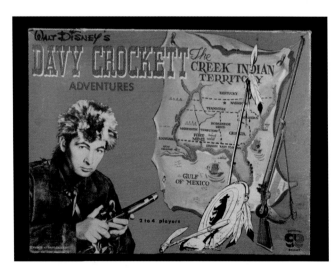

WALT DISNEY'S DAVY CROCKETT ADVENTURES
Gardner Games 1956
$45 - $65

WALT DISNEY'S DAVY CROCKETT ADVENTURES
Gardner Games 1956
Based on segments shown on ABC's DISNEYLAND TV show starring Fess Parker. Cool game includes large "Davy Crockett" spinner which pointed to colorful cards that players collected, such as "Davy battles Redstick" (an Indian), and "Davy grins the bear," whatever that means.

FESS PARKER WILDERNESS TRAIL CARD GAME
Transogram 1964
Fess Parker "as seen on the Daniel Boone Show." Simple card
game similar to "CINDERELLA" game of same year.
$25 - $35

ANNIE OAKLEY
Game Gems 1965
Based on the ABC TV show starring Gail Davis. Was originally
broadcast in the 1950s and is thought to be the first Western TV
series to star a woman. More plastic cowboys and Indians.
Courtesy of Rick Polizzi
$55 - $75

THE LEGEND OF JESSE JAMES
Milton Bradley 1966
Based on the movie.
$35 - $45

THE VIRGINIAN
Transogram 1962
"Adventures at Shiloh Ranch." Based on the NBC TV series
starring James Drury as "the Virginian," along with Lee J. Cobb,
Gary Clarke, and Doug McClure. Scarce game.
Courtesy of Rick Polizzi
$75 - $100

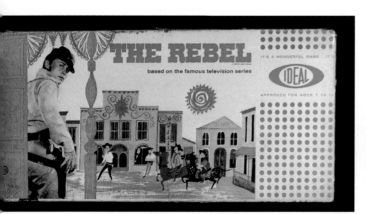

THE REBEL
Ideal 1961
Based on the ABC TV series starring Nick Adams.
Has neat plastic cowboys and Indians pieces.
$45 - $55

BUFFALO BILL JR'S CATTLE ROUND-UP
Built-Rite 1956
Based on TV series starring Dick Jones. Like all Built-Rite
games, it is cheesy and insubstantial, and has unrelated
"Horseshoe Derby Game" printed on reverse side of board.
A recent flood of this game, and the WILD BILL HICKOK'S
CAVALRY AND INDIANS GAME in mint unpunched condi-
tion, suggests a warehouse find and has lowered the price.
$20- $25

**WILD BILL HICKOK'S THE CAVALRY
AND THE INDIANS GAME**
Built-Rite 1956
Based on the TV series starring Guy Madison.
Reverse of board is "India" game.
Courtesy of Rick Polizzi
$20 - $25

WILD, WILD WEST
Transogram 1966
"The Frontier Agent Game." Based on the popular CBS TV series starring Robert
Conrad and Ross Martin. Extremely scarce and highly sought after game.
$350 - $550

THE DEPUTY
Milton Bradley 1960
Based on the TV series starring Henry Fonda. Came with
cool metal badge to be worn by winner of game.
$35 - $45

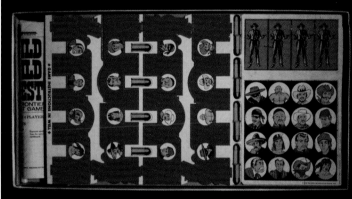

Inside of WILD, WILD WEST GAME.

THE RESTLESS GUN
Milton Bradley 1959
Based on NBC TV series starring John Payne. Game play and board
is exactly the same as SHOTGUN SLADE (see first book).
$35 - $45

BONANZA
Parker Brothers 1964
"As played by the Cartwrights at their Ponderosa Ranch."
Michigan Rummy game. Loosely, to say the least, based on
the NBC TV series starring Lorne Greene, Pernell Roberts,
Dan Blocker, and Michael Landon that ran for 15 years. In
fact, the only thing relating this to the Cartwrights is the
badly superimposed game on the table on the cover.
$25

RAWHIDE
Lowell 1960
Based on the CBS TV show starring Clint Eastwood and Eric Fleming. Game is sought after for the Clint Eastwood connection, but he does not appear on the cover.
$75 - $95

REWARD
HAPPY HOUR 1958
3-D Vacuformed game board, from same series as BILLIONAIRE and TICKY THE CLOWN CLOCK GAME (see first book). Another game that came with metal sheriff's badge.
$22 - $30

THE ADVENTURES OF RIN-TIN-TIN
Transogram 1955
Based on ABC TV series starring Lee Aaker as Rusty and Rin-Tin-Tin, although box states the game is based on "TV, Radio, and Movies."
$25 - $35

F TROOP
Ideal 1965
"Mini-Board Card Game." Based on the ABC TV series starring Forrest Tucker, Ken Berry and Larry Storch. From a series of small, simplistic "mini-board" games that Ideal put out that included I SPY, GET SMART, etc. (see first book).
$35 - $45

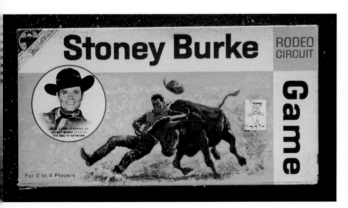

STONEY BURKE
Transogram 1963
"Rodeo Circuit" game. Based on the ABC TV series starring Jack Lord (of *HAWAII FIVE-0* fame). Players compete in four rodeo events.
$50 - $75

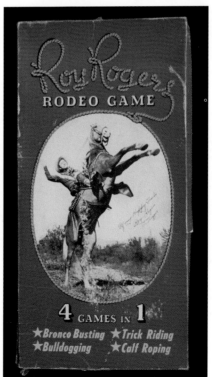

ROY ROGERS RODEO GAME
The Rogden Company 1949
Based on film and TV star Roy Rogers. Game has faux cover autograph of Roy Rogers and Trigger. His picture is in center of playing board. Plays similar to STONEY BURKE RODEO CIRCUIT GAME. However, the player who rolls the highest number on the dice at the beginning of the game gets to be "Roy." Rare game.
$125 - $250

9

COWBOYS AND INDIANS
Sam'l Gabriel Sons & Co. 1940s
"Build a corral, Capture a pony." Pretty much says it all. Small wooden sticks were inserted into the box bottom game board to "build a corral."
$20 - $25

"POW"
Selchow & Righter 1955
"The Frontier Game." From a children's series that included BUZZ, WASHOUT, and WUFFLE TREE. Cowboy and Indian game that ends in a "Battle to the death when the last man on either side is killed."
$15 - $22

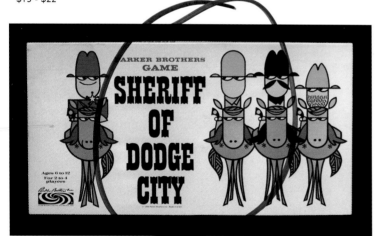

SHERIFF OF DODGE CITY
Parker Brothers 1966
$15 - $20

SEA RAIDER
Parker Brothers 1940s
"An exciting new game for young admirals."
Included metal ships.
$40 - $50

LITTLE CHIEF
Whitman 1960s
Came with neat paper headdresses.
$15

TEXAS RANGERS
All-Fair 1950s
Identical game (with similar cover) to All-Fair's 1956 game JACE PEARSON'S TALES OF THE TEXAS RANGERS (see first book). It's not clear which version came first.
$25 - $35

GUNFIGHT AT O.K. CORRAL
Ideal 1973
Large game in which players shoot at each other with ball-bearing firing guns. If your cowboy is hit, he pops off.
$25 - $35

DOVER PATROL
H.P. Gibson and Sons 1940s
"Or Naval Tactics." English game that included 80 ships on small metal stands.
$40 -$55

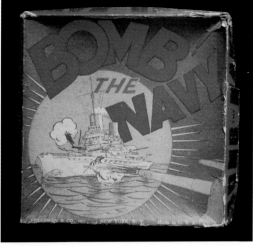

BOMB THE NAVY
J. Pressman & Co. 1940
Thin cardboard game includes five cardboard ships with stands. You roll glass marbles and try to knock over ships.
$30 - $45

BEACHHEAD INVASION
Built-Rite 1950s
Simple, but very large game. Unusual for this company.
$35 - $45

BOMBER BALL
Game Makers 1943
Cool skill and action game where "bombs" are dropped from cardboard airplane onto cardboard ship below.
$40 - $60

BATTLESHIP
Milton Bradley 1967
Original version of classic game (see first book for other versions). This cover is remembered by many as version where "the women" wash dishes in the kitchen while "the men" play war in the living room.
$15 - $20

SPOT-A-PLANE
Toy Creations 1942
2nd Edition. Eight different neat plastic planes are used in this "identification" game.
$35 - $45

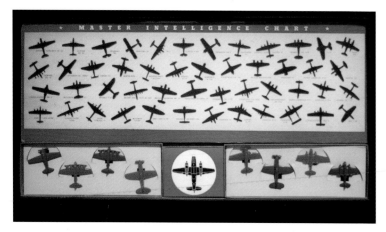

Inside of SPOT-A-PLANE.

OUR DEFENDERS
Master Toy Co. 1944
Assembly of four small puzzles of different soldiers is determined by spinner. Scarce.
$75 - $100

HOGAN'S HEROES
Transogram 1966
$125 - $150

BIZERTE GERTIE
Milton Bradley 1944
Rare wartime game involves soldiers trying to "meet and date exotic maids waiting in the park and stroll with them on the moonlit beach," such as Bizerte Gertie, Sally from Bali, and New Guinea Minnie. Loser gets stuck with "Alice the Hound Dog."
$100 - $125

HOGAN'S HEROES
Transogram 1966
"The Bluff Out Game." Based on CBS TV series starring Bob Crane. Scarce game has four different "Hogans" trying to collect Money, Passport and Map cards, to smuggle a prisoner out of the camp. Moves are determined by "color cards" which are selected by reaching into the "Hogan's Heroes Duffle Bag."

Above right:
FLYING ACES
Selchow & Righter 1940s
Metal airplanes.
$50 - $75

Right:
SALUTE!
Selchow & Righter 1942
Junior Edition. Patriotic game where at intervals players jump up and "salute" the 48 star flag that's included. A large box edition exists (see first book).
$50 - $75

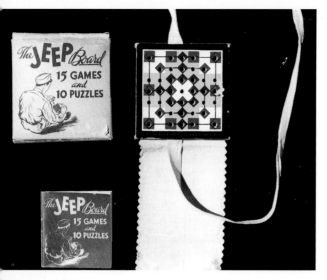

WATERLOO
Avalon Hill 1962
Very large version of
Napoleonic Campaign
strategy game.
$40 - $60

THE JEEP BOARD
George S. Carrington Co. 1943
Small game pack given to soldiers included 15 games and 10 puzzles. The
board had a cloth device that enabled the soldier to tie the game to his leg
so it wouldn't fall. A version by E.S. Lowe exists, valued at $20 - $30.
$25 - $40

STRATEGO
Milton Bradley 1961
Scarce "Fine Edition" of classic two handed military
game (see first book for other editions).
$25 - $30

U.S. SERVICE GAME KIT
Parker Brothers 1940s
Military issue of common
games (checkers, backgam-
mon, etc.).
$25 - $35

DICTATOR
Waltham Industries 1939
Very rare game in which
players use economic and
military powers to take over
countries. Tons of pieces.
Great Grand Daddy of RISK.
$500 - $600

CATCH A CHICKEN TORIE
Hasbro 1968
Revolutionary War theme. Ties with HEY PA! THERE'S A GOAT
ON THE ROOF for the worst title of a board game.
$22

TANK COMMAND
Ideal 1975
Large, super cool two player game involves manipulating under-the-board strings to blast your opponents plastic tanks.
$25 - $35

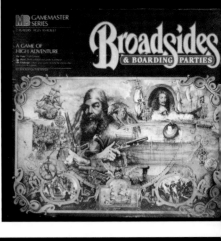

Right and below:
**BROADSIDES &
BOARDING PARTIES**
Milton Bradley 1984
$75 - $100

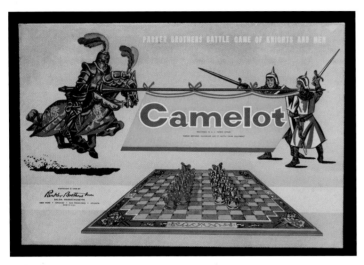

CAMELOT
Parker Brothers 1958
Yet another version of Parker Brother's classic game (see first book for other versions).
$25 - $30

**BROADSIDES &
BOARDING PARTIES**
Milton Bradley 1984
From the "Gamemaster Series" that included CONQUEST OF THE EMPIRE, AXIS & AL-LIES, and FORTRESS AMERICA (see first book). Players tried to either sink the enemy ship or capture the captain in this exciting game set in the 17th Century in the Caribbean. Featured two 15" tall plastic ships and 66 sailors, with cannons.

CAMELOT
Parker Brothers 1930
Beautiful cover painting of knights on this early version of "A Famous Game."
$40 - $60

PIRATES OF THE BARBARY COAST
1930s
"Stop the Corsairs, Get to Port Safely." Metal Ships.
$55 - $75

Everyone loves to make money, and board games catering to that primal urge have been around from very early on. From old standards like MONOPOLY and EASY MONEY to later variations such as CARTEL and THE AMERICAN DREAM, players have been given countless opportunities to display their business acumen. Remember, like it or not, money makes the world go round.

Bookshelf games are a unique variety of board game that blossomed during the 1960s and early 1970s. In most cases, a standard size game has been jammed into an 8 1/2" x 12" "book." The contents slide out of the slip cover box, and the game's name is printed on the spine of the exterior box. Put them on a shelf and they look like books. 3M was the leader in this field, along with Hasbro, Dynamic (Reiss) and Avalon Hill. 3M games have a strong following among collectors who value the game play as well as the odd sizes and shapes the games sometimes came in. In addition, rarities like JATI, a game that was never officially released, command high prices.

Board games about sports, or games emulating sports play, have always been enormously popular and, for the most part, valuable. The popularity of sports in today's culture has produced a whole class of sports collectors. Many of these enthusiasts cross over into board games. Games that have any connection to historic figures, such as BABE RUTH BASEBALL or JOHNNY UNITAS FOOTBALL, are highly sought after. On the other hand, because of the sheer number of sports games made over the years, many types and styles exist that are collectible, fun to play, AND affordable.

TYCOON
H.C. Jacoby Co. 1962
Stock Market simulation.
$25 - $35

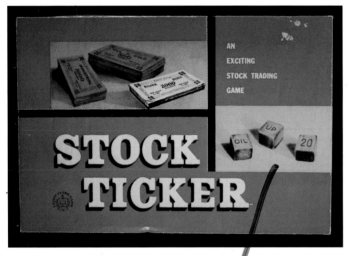

STOCK TICKER
Copp Clark 1950s
"An exciting Stock Trading game." Canadian. Money says
1937, but game seems to be from the 1950s.
$25 - $30

THE BIG BOARD
Milton Bradley 1937
"The game of Bankers and Brokers." Very large, very heavy
(ask the lady who sent it to me) game—pretty much sets up a
complicated stock exchange in your living room.
$55 - $75

TICKER
Glow Products, Inc. 1929
Unusually shaped stock market game includes chips and roll out
board. Valuable among collectors because it had the bad timing to be
released in the year of the great stock market crash. Rare.
$125 - $150

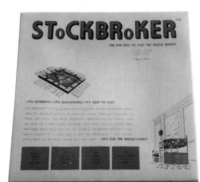

STOCKBROKER
Dow & Co. 1975
"The fun way to play the Stock
Market." Large elaborate board
with built in counters for changing
Stock Values during the game.
*Courtesy of Jeff Lowe's
ExtravaGAMEza*
$75 - $100

BULLS AND BEARS
Parker Brothers 1936
$100 - $150

BULLS AND BEARS
Parker Brothers 1936
"A Stock Exchange Game." This very rare stock market game featured lots of stock,
money, and 6 tiny metal "chairs" for the stock exchange. It was invented by Charles
B. Darrow (the "inventor" of MONOPOLY) and his signature and photograph
(showing MONOPOLY, ETC.) is prominently displayed on the box. The game sold
very poorly and is now hard to find. Since it's been proven that Darrow did not
actually invent MONOPOLY (he basically brought it to the attention of Parker
Brothers), it's not hard to believe that anything else he created might be unpopular.
I'd just like to know what the "Etc." refers to on the box, since I know of no other
games by Charles B. Darrow. (Game shown without board).

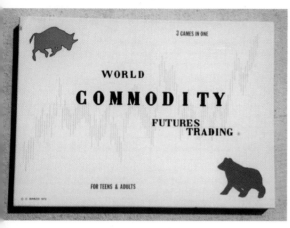

WORLD COMMODITY FUTURES TRADING
O. Bayazid 1972
Courtesy of Jeff Lowe's ExtravaGAMEza
$20 - $30

EASY MONEY
Milton Bradley 1935
This is the rare first edition of the game which included property "deeds," similar to MONOPOLY. After this version, the deeds were removed for all subsequent editions.
$100 - $150

CORNER THE MARKET
Atlantis Game Co. 1977
"The Commodity Trading Game."
Courtesy of Jeff Lowe's ExtravaGAMEza
$25 - $35

CENTRAL BANK
Right-On Mfg. 1974
"A Cunning, Baffling and Powerfully-Fun Game of Cards."
Unusual game container (money bag).
Courtesy of Jeff Lowe's ExtravaGAMEza
$15 - $20

EASY MONEY
Milton Bradley 1937
Early, unusual box design (see first book for other versions).
$25 - $35

DRIVE-IN
Selchow & Righter 1948
"The Money Making Movie Game." Super neat game involved booking movies, charging admission, and selling popcorn.
$50 - $75

BUY AND SELL
Whitman 1953
Pretty complicated game that had the kiddies buying and selling commodities "with play money."
$15 - $20

THE AMERICAN DREAM
Milton Bradley 1979
"Buy stock in famous companies, patent your inventions,
buy franchises, and make a million!" Large game.
$20 - $25

PAYDAY
Payday Game Co. 1975
"The People's Game."
Courtesy of Jeff Lowe's ExtravaGAMEza
$20 - $30

NATIONAL LAMPOON GAME OF SELLOUT
Cardinal Industries 1983
"The totally unethical, incredibly realistic game of making
it to the top." From the irreverent humor magazine.
$20

EXPANSE
Milton Bradley 1949
"A Globe Trotting Game of Fun and Fortune." Rare game
had players traveling the world to make their fortune.
From the collection of Bob Claster
$30 - $45

FINANCE
Parker Brothers 1936
This rare game, the same as FINANCE AND FORTUNE, was issued
under this name in 1936. This title resurfaced again in 1958 (see first
book). It all had to do with Parker Brothers acquiring the rights to Knapp
Electric's FINANCE and other MONOPOLY related sleight-of-hand.
$40 - $65

FINANCE
Knapp Electric, Inc. 1932
(Shown without game board). Very rare, one of the predecessors (along with THE
LANDLORD'S GAME) of MONOPOLY. Has the all important Property Deeds, as
well as weird shaped houses, hotels, Chance and Community Chest cards. In this
game, all the Community Chest cards *help* the Community, i.e. "Pay American
Legion $1," "Pay Red Cross $50," etc., as opposed to rewarding the player.
$250 - $300

Closeup of Knapp Electric FINANCE Hotel and House

20

CHAIRMAN OF THE BOARD
Mocomo Co. 1975
Courtesy of Jeff Lowe's ExtravaGAMEza
$20 - $25

SYNDICATES
JGA Enterprises 1978
"The Big Money Game of Business."
Courtesy of Jeff Lowe's ExtravaGAMEza
$20 - $25

VEGAS
Hasbro 1969
$25 - $30

CARTEL
Gamut of Games 1974
"Build a Worldwide Billion $ Empire." 2nd Edition. Sought after game, reissued in 1985 as DALLAS (see first book).
From the collection of Bob Claster
$50 - $75

VEGAS
Hasbro 1969
Part of Hasbro's NBC "At Home Entertainment" series that included WALLSTREET, RHYME TIME, INTERPRETATION OF DREAMS, MOB STRATEGY, MATING GAME, IT TAKES TWO, CHAIN LETTERS, and TRIVIA (see first book). Players land at Vegas Airport with ten million dollars in cash and start gambling, buying up hotels, and generally try to shaft the other players. Quite a bit of fun material is jammed into a small box.

PROFIT OR LOSS
Hollow Stump Bungalow Books & Games 1977
"$2,500 can make you a Millionaire."
Courtesy of Jeff Lowe's ExtravaGAMEza
$20 - $30

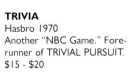

TRIVIA
Hasbro 1970
Another "NBC Game." Forerunner of TRIVIAL PURSUIT.
$15 - $20

JATI
3M 1965
Extremely rare game. Apparently 100 test copies were made, but feedback showed the game wasn't very good, so it never made it into mass production. 3M collectors have paid record prices for the game.
From the collection of Bob Claster
$1200 - $2000

BACKGAMMON
3M 1973
Uncommon game for 3M.
From the collection of Bob Claster
$20 - $25

AIRPORT
Dynamic 1972
Air Traffic Controlling.
$15 - $20

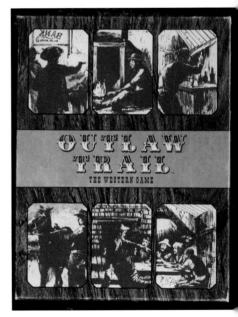

CHESS
3M 1970
Very nice pieces.
From the collection of Bob Claster
$25 - $30

GO
3M 1974
From the collection of Bob Claster
$20 - $25

OUTLAW TRAIL
Dynamic 1972
Dynamic produced a whole series of games in the 1970s such as SOCIETY TODAY, THE FAMILY GAME, and BEAT DETROIT (see first book).
$15 - $20

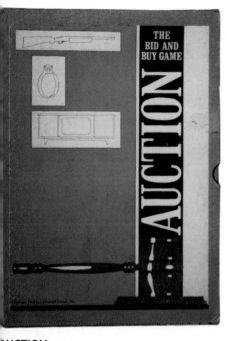

AUCTION

Universal Games 1965

"The Bid and Buy Game." Actually a neat game where players bid on all kinds of weird things.

$20 - $25

EVENTS

3M 1974

"The what, where and when game." Common.

From the collection of Bob Claster

$10 - $15

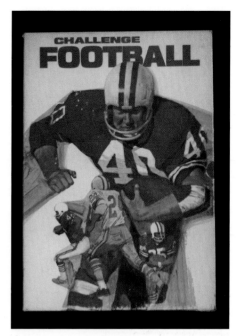

CHALLENGE FOOTBALL

3M 1972

From a series that included sports such as Golf.

From the collection of Bob Claster

$20 -$25

ESP

Dynamic Games 1972

"The Game of Perceptive Skill." Cross between ESP and Psychoanalysis.

$25 - $30

CONTIGO

3M 1974

From the collection of Bob Claster

$15 - $20

BID & BLUFF

3M 1972

Rare game in uncommon container from 3M. Dice and card game.

From the collection of Bob Claster

$75 - $150

MIMIKRI
3M 1970s?
3M collectors love the weird, uncommon stuff from this company. This German chess version has a beautiful board and pieces.
From the collection of Bob Claster
$25 - $35

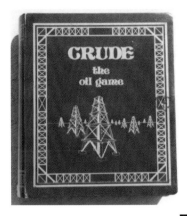

CRUDE
St. Laurent Games 1974
"The oil game." Large bookshelf game highly valued by game players. Later recycled into a German game called MCMULTI (which is also highly prized).
Courtesy of Jeff Lowe's ExtravaGAMEza
$300 - $400

HIGH-BID
3M 1970
$15 -$20

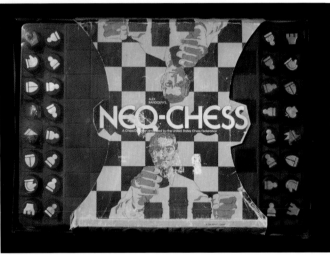

NEO-CHESS
3M 1972
Another bizarre 3M chess variation.
From the collection of Bob Claster
$50 - $75

HIGH-BID
3M 1970
In 1970, 3M made a series of small card game versions of some of their bookshelf games and called them "Gamettes." They were about the size of a small paperback, and opened as a book does. Again, they managed to pack all the fun of the larger size version into an even smaller space. 3M collectors try to gather the whole series (see first book for full size version of HIGH-BID).

OCTRIX
3M 1969
In 1968-69, 3M adapted some of their Bookshelf games into card games packed in "butter dishes." The series included TRYCE, VENTURE, and others (see first book). OCTRIX is rare.
From the collection of Bob Claster
$75 - $100

OCTRIX
3M 1970
Same as the "Butter Dish" version.
From the collection of Bob Claster
$45 - $55

MONAD
3M 1970
"Action game of buying and trading." Strange "Ying /Yang" symbols were the tokens.
From the collection of Bob Claster
$20 - $25

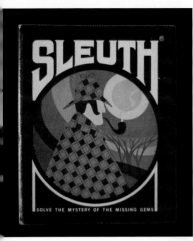

SLEUTH
3M 1971
Inventor Sid Sackson sold this game
concept to Ideal in 1967 and it
became part of their "Famous
Mystery Classic Series," including
THE CASE OF THE ELUSIVE
ASSASSIN: AN ELLERY QUEEN
MYSTERY GAME (see first book).
$15 - $20

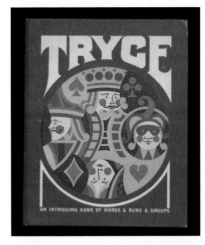

TRYCE
3M 1970
"Butter Dish" version exists
(see first book).
*From the collection of Bob
Claster*
$25 - $30

VENTURE
3M 1970
"Butter Dish" versions were made
(see first book).
From the collection of Bob Claster
$15 - $20

PRO BOWL LIVE ACTION FOOTBALL
Marx 1969
HUGE game with large plastic players, playing
field, goal posts, and a motorized runner!
$40 - $50

EVADE
3M 1970
Naval maneuver game.
From the collection of Bob Claster
$20 - $25

FOIL
3M 1970
Players form words and unscramble
opponents words.
From the collection of Bob Claster
$15 - $20

PIGSKIN
Parker Brothers 1960
In the 1930s and 40s, this game was known as
TOM HAMILTON'S PIGSKIN FOOTBALL.
$25 - $35

ROSE BOWL
Keck Enterprises 1949
Emil "Red" Sitko, Howard Odell, and Jeff
Cravath all give it thumbs up, whoever they are.
$35 - $45

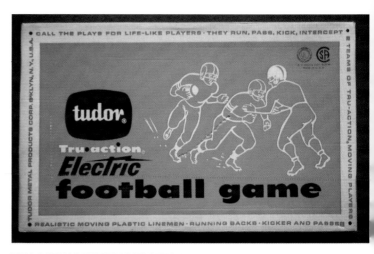

TRU-ACTION ELECTRIC FOOTBALL
Tudor 1960s
Everyone remembers this electric game where all the plastic players wiggle
around and fall over. It was made forever, and has little value.
$15 - $20

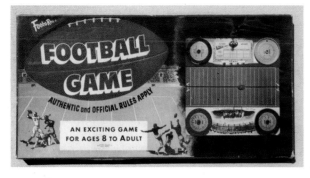

FOOBA-ROU FOOTBALL
Memphis Plastic Ent. 1955
Combination of Football and Roulette.
Courtesy of Jeff Lowe's ExtravaGAMEza
$35 - $45

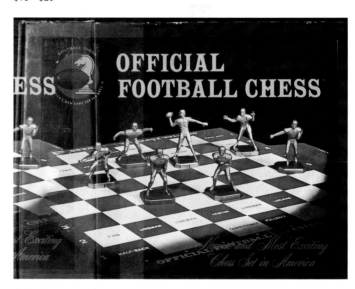

OFFICIAL FOOTBALL CHESS
Neiden, Winton and Ass. 1967
Another giant, plastic football game, but
this time it's a neat chess set.
$40 - $50

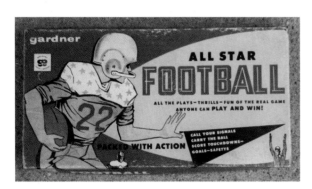

ALL STAR FOOTBALL
Gardner 1950s
From a sports series that included CHAMPION-
SHIP GOLF and others (see first book).
Courtesy of Jeff Lowe's ExtravaGAMEza
$20 - $30

Inside of OFFICIAL FOOTBALL CHESS.

OOTBALL
Pressman 1930s
reat stylized football "players" on cover.
ourtesy of Jeff Lowe's ExtravaGAMEza
40 -$50

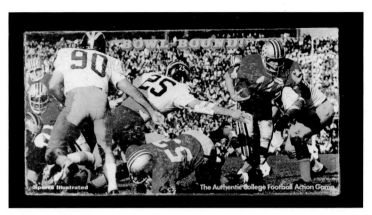

BOWL BOUND
Sports Illustrated 1973
Another "Authentic College Football Action Game."
Courtesy of J. Hardy
$20 - $25

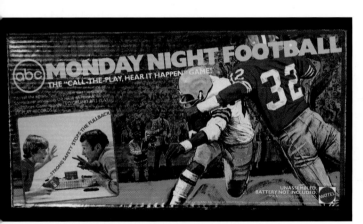

ALKING ABC MONDAY NIGHT FOOTBALL
attel 1977
cluded "Voice Unit" and 13 play-by-play records. Originally
eleased as TALKING FOOTBALL (see first book).
35 - $45

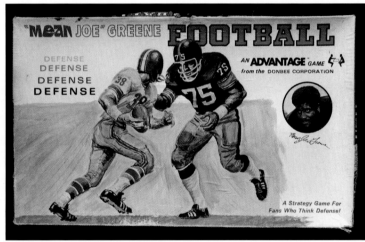

"MEAN JOE" GREENE FOOTBALL
Advantage 1974
Obscure "Defense" game of football personality "Mean Joe" Greene.
$35 - $45

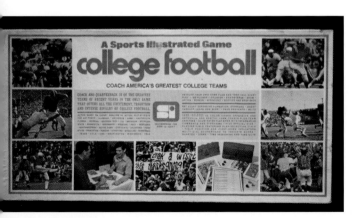

OLLEGE FOOTBALL
ports Illustrated 1972
Coach America's Greatest College Teams." *Sports Illustrated* put
ut a variety of games in the 1970s, such as BOWL BOUND,
RACK MEET, and GO FOR THE GREEN! (see first book).
20 - $25

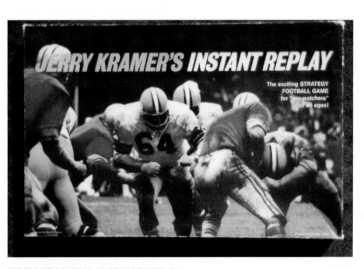

JERRY KRAMER'S INSTANT REPLAY
EMD Enterprises 1970
Rare. $30 - $40

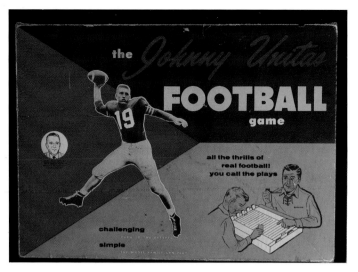

JOHNNY UNITAS FOOTBALL
Play-Rite 1960
Very rare game of legendary football personality Johnny Unitas.
$150 - $200

ELMER LAYDEN'S SCIENTIFIC FOOTBALL
Cadaco-Ellis 1942
"College Edition."
$55 - $75

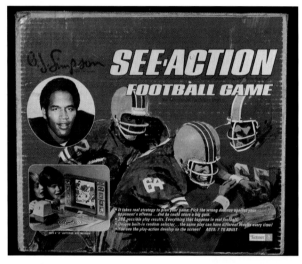

O.J. SIMPSON SEE-ACTION FOOTBALL
Kenner 1974
Unusual "small box" version of rare game (see first book)
$250 - $350

OFFICIAL RADIO BASEBALL
Toy Creations 1940
They had a series of "Official" games that included Basketball and Hockey.
$30 - $40

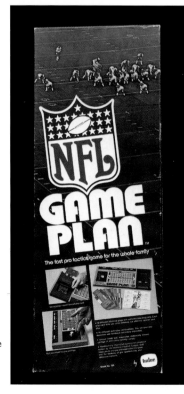

NFL GAME PLAN
Tudor 1972
Rare non-electric football game made by the electric football company.
$25 - $30

HANK AARON BASEBALL
Ideal 1973
Same game as SURE SHOT BASEBALL put out by Ideal in 1970.
$25 - $35

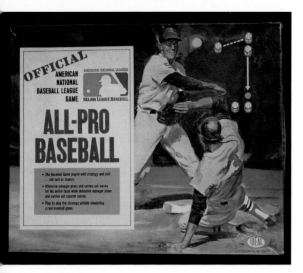

ALL-PRO BASEBALL
Ideal 1969
The large, "Official" All-Pro series included Basketball,
Football, and Hockey (see first book).
$35 - $40

LITTLE LEAGUE BASEBALL
Standard Toykraft 1964
Rare entry from a company that made very few games. Created to
celebrate the 25th Anniversary of Little League Baseball.
$35 - $45

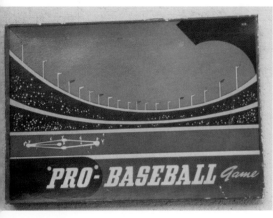

PRO-BASEBALL
Toy Creations 1940
Before OFFICIAL RADIO BASEBALL.
Courtesy of Jeff Lowe's ExtravaGAMEza
$50 - $75

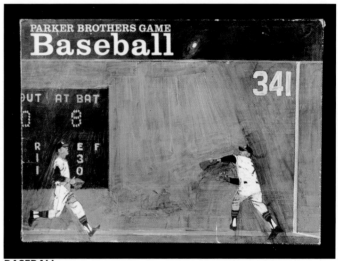

BASEBALL
Parker Brothers 1967
Beautiful cover.
$25 - $30

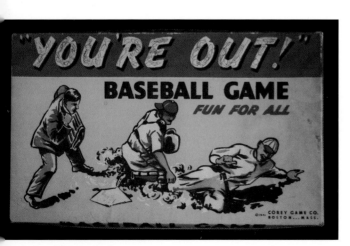

YOU'RE OUT! BASEBALL GAME
Corey Games 1941
Simple skill and action game.
$20 - $30

LONG SHOT
Parker Brothers 1962
Obscure horse racing game.
$20 - $25

BROADWAY HANDICAP
Official Films 1950s
Six different 16mm motion picture films of horse races could be projected on a screen, each with a different outcome. Set included Odds book, money, and wagering forms. Could be purchased in 8mm and 16mm with sound.
$30 - $45

HOC-KEY
Cadaco-Ellis 1958
Basically same game as BAS-KET (see first book).
$35 - $45

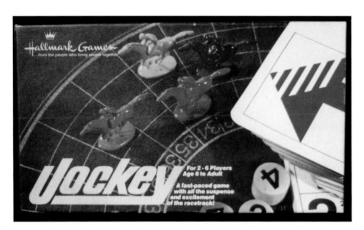

JOCKEY
Hallmark Games 1976
Horse race game. Actually an import by Ravensburger.
From the collection of Bob Claster
$20 - $25

BAS-KET
Cadaco 1973
Harlem Globetrotters Official Edition. This same game was recycled again in 1980 for THE WHITE SHADOW.
$25 - $35

BAS-KET
Cadaco-Ellis 1938
Very early game by this company, changed very little over the next 40 years.
$75 - $85

SPEED BOAT RACE
Milton Bradley 1930s
Courtesy of Jeff Lowe's ExtravaGAMEza
$50 - $75

CLIPPER RACE
Samuel Gabriel & Sons
1930s
Large game with cover painting by Gordon Grant (Homeward She Drives). Object is to be the first to sail your ship to Shanghai, China, and back.
$125 - $150

VERNE GAGNE WORLD CHAMPION WRESTLING
Gardner 1950s
"As seen on TV." Apparently Verne was a Wrestling star in the 1950s. Four die-cut wrestling figures fought their way to the center ring using the included "Wrestling Holds and Regulations" booklet and the wrestling holds spinner (which included holds like "The Cobra Twist," "Flying Mares," and the "Back Breaker"). The first player landing by exact count in the center ring got the Champion Belt and was the winner. Rare game.

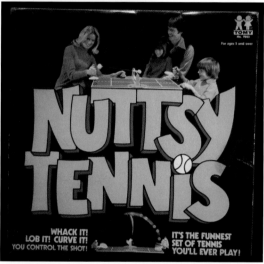

CHAMPIONSHIP FIGHT GAME
Frankie Goodman 1940s
Courtesy of Jeff Lowe's ExtravaGAMEza
$50 - $75

NUTTSY TENNIS
Tomy 1974
Upside down Ping-Pong paddles whack the tethered ball back and forth. Neat game!
$10 - $15

ERNE GAGNE WORLD CHAMPION WRESTLING
ardner 1950s
55 - $200

SAMSONITE BAS-KETBALL
Samsonite 1969
Large game. There was also a SAMSONITE PRO FOOTBALL (see first book).
$25 - $35

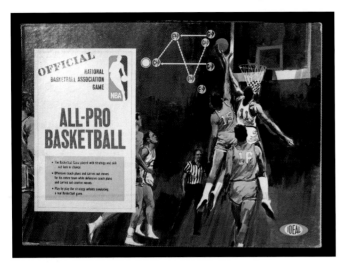

ALL-PRO BASKETBALL
Ideal 1969
Large game from Ideal series (see first book).
$35 - $40

TEST DRIVER
Milton Bradley 1956
"At the Chrysler Corp. Proving Grounds." The Chrysler connection
has auto collectors driving the price of this game.
$75 - $125

JIM PRENTICE ELECTRIC BASKETBALL
Electric Game Co. 1949
Early game had light up bulbs to score points. Other
electric games included ELECTRIC BASEBALL,
ELECTRIC FOOTBALL, and ELECTRIC HOCKEY.

RACE-A-WAY
Milton Bradley 1973
"Championship Auto Race Game." Muscle cars on the cover of this game.
$20 - $25

OLYMPIAD
Everon International 1977
Scarce game
Courtesy of Jeff Lowe's ExtravaGAMEza
$30 - $35

COLLISION!
Whitman 1969
Demolition derby race.
$20 - $25

HUGGIN' THE RAIL
Selchow & Righter 1958
Scarce version of game with "updated" cover. Why
try to improve on the original? (See first book).
$30 - $35

LE MANS
Avalon Hill 1961
Early racing simulation.
$25 - $35

POWER 4 CAR RACING GAME
Manning Mfg. 1960s
Large game came with plastic cars and a large
motorized spinner that spun colored marbles.
Where the marbles landed determined your move.
Courtesy of Jeff Lowe's ExtravaGAMEza
$40 - $55

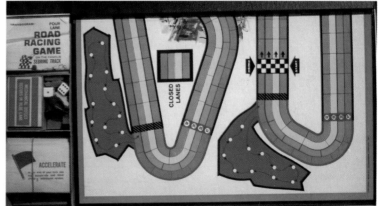

STRAIGHTAWAY
Selchow & Righter 1961
Based on the TV Series. The only game based on TV done by this company.
Courtesy of Rick Polizzi
$55 - $75

KAR-ZOOM
Whitman 1964
Pretty lame game consisted of flicking a disc
(as in shuffleboard) into the point area.
$20 - $25

Inside of FOUR LANE ROAD RACING.

FOUR LANE ROAD RACING
Transogram 1963
"On the Famous Sebring Track." Let's face it, the cover gives the distinct impression
that they're racing model cars, which was the fad at the time. They're not.
$30 - $40

AUTO DROME
Transogram 1967
Uses same concept as AURORA DERBY.
$25 - $35

FLYING SAUCER HORSESHOE GAME
Wamo 1950s
This set was put out when Wham-O Frisbees were still
called "Pluto Platters." Early, rare game.
$50 - $75

**ROSCOE TURNER AIR RACE
GAME**
Southern Games 1960
He looks like "Wrong-Way Corrigan" to
me. Rare game.
Courtesy of Jeff Lowe's ExtravaGAMEza
$125 - $150

HOME GOLF
Mel Weiss Ent. 1961
$75 - $85

X-C CROSS COUNTRY
Krieg Brand Products 1969
"Win a flying cross country race!" Cool plastic airplanes.
$30 - $40

HOME GOLF
Mel Weiss Ent. 1961
Huge, rare golf set included eighteen "holes," a full set of plastic clubs,
Styrofoam ball, scorecards, and large putting green with built-in cup.
Mom seems mystified by the whole process. One of the nicer attempts
to bring the experience of golf inside "the comfort of your living room."

SHUFFLES
Aurora 1969
"The Table-top Shuffleboard Game." Very large mechanical
game is really cool. Scarce game by company that made few.
$40 - $50

STRIKE
Hasbro 1950s
Obscure bowling game.
Courtesy of Jeff Lowe's ExtravaGAMEza
$25 - $30

JUNIOR TABLE TOP BOWLING ALLEY
Merit 1961
"As Advertised in *Life*."
$40 - $50

WHIZ BOWL
Zenith Toy Corp. 1950s
This and Pee Dee's 1958 HIT AND TOUCH MECHANICAL BOWL-
ING GAME are the forerunners of SKITTLE BOWL (see first book).
Courtesy of Jeff Lowe's ExtravaGAMEza
$20 - $30

SPARE-TIME
Spare-Time 1960s
Small game in which special dice came
in plastic bowling pin container.
$10 - $15

GALLOPING GOLF
Bee-Line Products 1950s
Dice golf game.
$15 - $20

BOWLING CARD GAME
Ed-U-Cards 1962
Similar to BOWLO (see first book).
$5 - $7

LIGHT HORSE HARRY COOPER'S GOLF GAME
Trojan Games 1943
Courtesy of Jeff Lowe's ExtravaGAMEza
$150 - $200

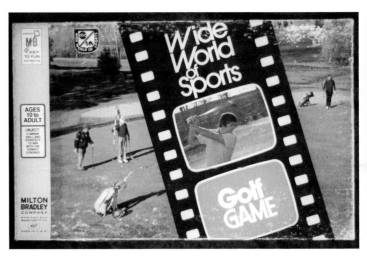

WIDE WORLD OF SPORTS GOLF GAME
Milton Bradley 1975
Game series included Auto Racing and Tennis.
$25 - $30

BING CROSBY'S INDOOR RETURN-A-PUTT
Bing's Things 1959
Large plastic mound returns balls automatically (if you putt into the mound).
$40 - $50

BIRDIE GOLF
Barris Corp. 1964
Rare game.
Courtesy of Jeff Lowe's ExtravaGAMEza
$50 - $75

JACK NICKLAUS PRACTICE MAT
Dynaball Corp. 1960s
"Approved and Endorsed by Jack Nicklaus."
$25 - $35

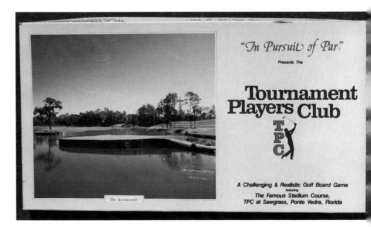

IN PURSUIT OF PAR
Pursuit of Par Co. 1988
Game emulates the TPC at Sawgrass, Ponte Vedra, Florida.
$20 - $25

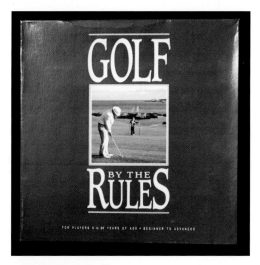

GOLF BY THE RULES
J.D. Golf Rules, Inc. 1990
Trivia game that teaches golf rules.
$10 - $15

GOLFERINO
Hubley 1963
A *real* miniature golf game. You control a golfer who tries to putt up bridges, through tunnels, and around corners to win the "Loving Cup"... which pops out of the last hole. This rare game was re-released years later by another company and called PIVOT GOLF. The only other game this company made is the much sought after JUNGLE HUNT.
$175 - $250

OFF COURSE
Slade, Inc. 1986
$15 - $20

Closeup of GOLFERINO.

MINI GOLF
Tudor 1960s
"Snap Action" helped you propel the "ball" into the different miniature golf style holes in this scarce game. From a small series of large "snap action" sports games.
$25 - $35

Remco Industries, Inc. was started in 1949 by two young men in their mid-twenties, Issac Heller and Saul Robbins. Their New Jersey based "factory" (they employed one other person beside themselves in the beginning) exploited a new-fangled discovery whose properties were just beginning to be appreciated: plastics. They made toys, "Walkie-Talkie" toys to be precise; but, they would eventually grow into one of the country's biggest toy manufacturers.

The battery operated "Big Plastic" toys they made, like the SCREAMING MEE-MEE GUN, WHIRLYBIRD HELICOPTER, FIGHTING LADY BATTLESHIP, FIREBIRD-99 DASHBOARD, FLYING FOX AIRLINER and the whole MONKEY DIVISION and HAMILTON INVADERS series excited a whole generation of kids from the 1950s through the 1960s. They were one of the first toy companies to realize the power of television, and they advertised heavily. Though inelegant, their slogan "EVERY BOY WANTS A REMCO TOY... AND SO DO GIRLS" is emblazoned in the minds of a million children who sat glued to the tube in those early years.

Toys were their thing, but they also made board games. An[d] although they made few games, they now occupy their own nich[e] in board games collecting.

The company's first games seem to have been made in 1958, [as] part of the "Giant Wheel" series. These games came in large, coars[e] cardboard boxes, but the covers were printed with delightfully sim[ple] plistic cartoon drawings that were very appealing. The "Giant Whee[l]" was a large plastic (of course) "wheel-of-fortune" type device th[at] the players would put together and set up. Once assembled, the whe[el] was spun. A small piece of plastic at the top of the wheel made th[e] "klak-klak" sound of a playing card attached to a bicycle wheel's spok[e] as it revolved. The number or icon it pointed to gave the amount [of] position that the player moved his piece.

The playing board was unique in that it was a very large (almost [?] feet long!) colorful playing "mat" that remained rolled up when not [in] use. Depending on the game, the moving pieces could be plastic cov[boy] boys and Indians, horses, cars, or race boats. Some of the games cam[e] with other plastic pieces or cards that augmented play.

Games from this series included GIANT WHEEL COWBOYS AND INDIANS, GIANT WHEEL THRILLS AND SPILLS HORSE RACE GAME, GIANT WHEEL OLD MAID, GIANT WHEEL BINGO, GIANT WHEEL MISSISSIPPI SPEED BOAT RACE and GIANT WHEEL HOT ROD SPORT CAR RACE.

I guess the next logical step from a device that acts like a pair of dice IS a pair of dice, and the next series was called TUMBLEBUM DICE. These games were built exactly the same as the GIANT WHEEL series except, instead of the wheel, a large plastic dice cage (similar to ones in ritzy chuck-a-luck casino games) was used. Players spun this from the handles on the sides, and took their movements from the die. The games from this series included NOTCH, SHMO and MELVIN THE MOON MAN. In addition, these three games were sold together in a very rare "COMBINATION DICE GAME" for a short period.

A series of games in a much smaller size came out in the very early sixties with names like FLAPJACK, and HOT POTATO. These were very simple skill-and-action games that relied on plastic pieces, whether they be "flapjacks" or "potatoes." At the same time, a similar sized series came out that had small plastic playing boards. These were traditional "track" games (players moving their pawns around a track, from beginning to end), with small plastic playing pieces and, sometimes, decks of cards. This series is hard to find, and included PINHEAD, KICK THE CAN, DOUBLE OR NOTHIN' and JOHNNY ON THE PONY. Again, the simple art is beautiful.

Then, in 1961, Remco developed a skill and action game that was to become one of the biggest selling games of its day: FASCINATION. FASCINATION stayed a big seller for the company all the way through 1969. The game consisted of two double-sided plastic mazes that were attached to two battery-operated light towers. The two players each had 3 metal balls that they tried to coerce through the plastic maze and into the three final slots. The first player to accomplish this would have his tower light up with his color (red or blue), and he would be declared the winner. Very simple, but it took the game community by storm. A spin-off called HIPPOPOTAMUS (with an electric "puzzle") was introduced, as well as blatant attempts to copy their own success with games called FASCINATION POOL and FASCINATION CHECKERS. Neither of these latter games were electric, nor were they nearly as much fun. Another game, called FRUSTRATION BALL, appeared and, although neat, faded into obscurity after lackluster sales.

In 1962, it appears the company started to experiment with licensing existing characters, and produced an amazing battery operated toy for Gerry Anderson's SUPERCAR television show, based on the car itself. Toys were created for other TV shows in 1964, such as THE MUNSTERS and VOYAGE TO THE BOTTOM OF THE SEA, as well as a series of dolls based on THE BEATLES.

However, the first board games from this period seem to come from 1965 with games based on the hit music shows HULLA BALOO and SHINDIG. A doll Remco developed, called Heidi, got her own game called HEIDI ELEVATOR GAME. These games were very simply made, and without much substance. They were the same size and shape as most board games, with a folding game board and cardboard die cut pawns to move around.

The company seemed to switch to super heroes in 1966, with toys based on BATMAN and THE GREEN HORNET, although they did create one of the most desirable games of any era, the LOST IN SPACE 3-D SPACE GAME. This extremely rare game had a game board constructed in three dimensions, with plastic spacemen playing pieces moving from one level to the next.

From there the company seems to have given up on board games until the last two years of the 1960s. In 1968-69, Remco produced games based on the television shows HAWAII FIVE-0, THE MOD SQUAD, THAT GIRL, FAMILY AFFAIR, LANCER and the completely obscure ABC mystery show, JOURNEY TO THE UNKNOWN. An "Electric Quiz" series also included CHITTY CHITTY BANG BANG, based on the movie.

All of the board games Remco produced are scarce, but those from this last effort represent some of the rarest and hardest to find of any games. As such, their worth is high. Collectors value them not only for the popularity (or lack of popularity) of the shows involved, but for their incredible scarcity.

Remco continued to produce a few games here and there after this period, like BOP BASEBALL, SPORTS ELECTRIC QUIZ, MYSTERY ZODIAC, MONKEY AUTO RACES, and THE MAGIC MAGIC MAGIC GAME; but the 1970s were hard for Remco and all toy companies. In the seventies, Remco sold out to Azrak/Hamway.

Remco may not have made a lot of games, but the ones they DID make left a lasting impression on many boys...and girls too!

HOT ROD
Remco 1960
$65 - $75

HOT ROD
Remco 1960
"The Sport Car Race." All the "Giant Wheel" games came with a large rolled mat which served as the playing board, and the 12" tall Giant Wheel. Spinning the wheel determined your movement on the board. Cool plastic "hot rods" raced around the track, avoiding spinouts and crashes. This particular set is probably the hardest to find of the Giant Wheel series.

OLD MAID
Remco 1960
A cross between the card game Old Maid and bingo. Plastic chips were placed on your section of the play mat in accordance to the figures on the "Giant Wheel." Avoid the large plastic Old Maid card. Hard to find set. $35 - $45

Inside of OLD MAID.

MISSISSIPPI
Remco 1960
"The Speed Boat Race." Similar to HOT ROD except the Giant Wheel directed plastic speed boats around the board, hopefully avoiding trouble and seeking the finish line. Uncommon in the series. $55 - $65

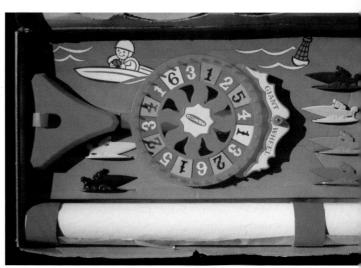

Inside of MISSISSIPPI.

GIANT WHEEL THRILLS' N SPILLS HORSE RACE
Remco 1958
THRILLS 'N SPILLS and GIANT WHEEL COWBOYS AND INDIANS were Remco's first games. Straight-forward horse racing game, except the Giant Wheel determined the moves. Plastic horses were used as well as plastic "wooden" steeplechase fences. The cover gives the impression that the game is three-dimensional, but it's the same flat mat playing board. Instructions were on the bottom of the box for these two games, the first and last time Remco did this.
Courtesy of Rick Polizzi
$35 - $45

Inside of THRILLS' N SPILLS HORSE RACE.

GIANT WHEEL COWBOYS AND INDIANS
Remco 1958

Remco's "other" first game. Plastic Cowboy and Indian pieces. The plastic fences are now "corrals" and fences around the Indian village. The Giant Wheel controls the moves and players can leap over fences to take short-cuts. It's interesting that the object for the Indians is to get home to their village, while the object for the cowboys is to go to jail.

$50 - $55

Inside of COWBOYS AND INDIANS.

Not shown: **GIANT WHEEL PICTURE BINGO**, Remco 1960.
$25 - $35

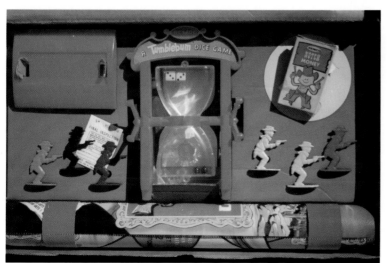

SHMO
Remco 1959

Remco next created the "Tumblebum Dice" series, where the "Giant Wheel" was replaced by a very large plastic dice cage. The cage was spun and the dice tumbled down. The large playing pieces and huge rolled mat continued. In this baffling game, the kid who lands on a Shmo space (which shows the shmo going to school without his pants or pouring salt into his Dad's coffee) takes a shmo card and performs whatever weird activity is called for on the card. Mercifully, the object is to **not** be a shmo.
$35 - $45

NOTCH
Remco 1960

Large plastic cowboy playing pieces. The Tumblebum told you your moves. You went around the board doing good deeds (saving schoolmarm on runaway horse, stopping bank holdup). By doing this, you'd get "notches." In the end, the notches are converted into "notch money." The one with the most money wins. I have no idea how kids would have kept track of how many notches they had earned through the course of the game.
$40 - $50

Inside of NOTCH.

MELVIN THE MOON MAN
Remco 1959
Large plastic spacemen. Similar to NOTCH, only instead of getting "notches" for good deeds, you get "moon bucks" for ripping-off the Moon Men. The Tumblebum directs you in trading your camera for moon bucks or selling views of the earth through a telescope. To reach the finish, you can either bribe Melvin or take the long way around.
$55 - $65

FLAPJACK
Remco 1959
More toy than game, players flipped plastic flapjacks. Depending where they landed, players give or take flapjacks away.
$25 - $35

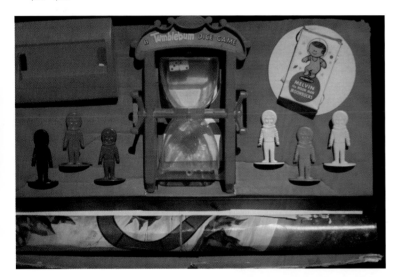

Inside of FLAPJACK.

Inside of MELVIN THE MOON MAN.

HOT POTATO
Remco 1959
Players hid the hot potato in one of the four pots, and cards told them which pot to take from whom. Game included an old-time clock windup timer.
$25 - $35

side of HOT POTATO.

Above right and right:
KICK THE CAN
Remco 1959
"A Great Old Game." Pretty lame game which had a plastic spring loaded "shoe" kicking the dice. That's it. There were only 21 spaces in the whole game! It's interesting to note that Remco used a different artist for the outside and inside of their games. I much prefer the simplified elegance of the outside covers on all their games to the garish heavy-handed "comic book" style on the inside.
$25 - $35

DOUBLE OR NOTHIN'
Remco 1959
"The Follow the Leader Game." In the late fifties Remco started this series of small, simple games. Each included a small plastic game board, small plastic moving pieces and cards or dice. A far cry from the giant Tumblebum and Giant Wheel games. In this game players advanced down a path picking cards which would double their dice roll or give them nothin'.
30

side of DOUBLE OR NOTHIN'.

PINHEAD
Remco 1959
"The Game of Hide and Seek." Simple track game, but one of the weirdest covers they put out (giving the impression that you're playing *LAND OF THE GIANTS*).
$25 - $30

JOHNNY ON THE PONY

Remco 1959
"The On Again, Off Again Game." Game included cute little plastic "Johnny" and "Pony" pieces. Players flipped a Johnny/Pony coin to determine which card stack they choose from. First player to stay mounted on his pony and reach the finish won.
$40 -$45

Inside of JOHNNY ON THE PONY.

FASCINATION

Remco 1961
This was a different box style put out the same year.
$25

FASCINATION

Remco 1968
This photo box cover was the last incarnation by the company.
$30

FASCINATION

Remco 1961
Original box. This was Remco's big hit. Players tried to maneuver three metal balls through plastic mazes in an attempt to be the first to light up his or her colored light. Simple, but very Fascinating...
$25 - $35

FASCINATION CHECKERS

Remco 1962
Remco attempts to cash in on the success of FASCINATION. The only thing fascinating about this Chinese Checkers variant was the name.
$20 - $25

Inside of FASCINATION CHECKERS.

ASCINATION POOL
emco 1962
nother game fashioned after FASCINATION. Players attempt to put different
olored balls into same colored pockets simultaneously. But nothing lights up.
20 - $25

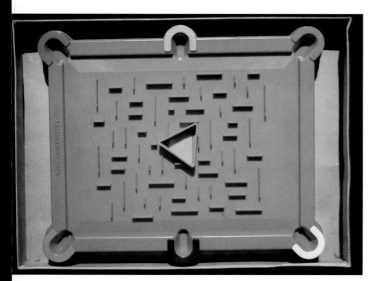

side of FASCINATION POOL.

HIPPOPOTAMUS
Remco 1961
Electric game using the same colored light system to determine the winner; but, this game uses the completion of simple puzzles as the race, not marbles in mazes. A similar system was used in HULLABALOO ELECTRIC TEEN GAME in 1965.
$25 - $35

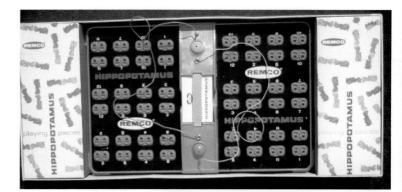

Inside of HIPPOPOTAMUS.

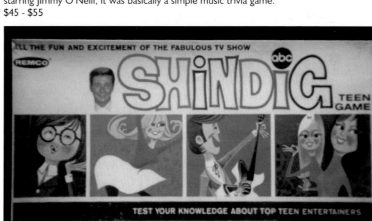

FRUSTRATION BALL
Remco 1969
This nasty entry came late in the game for Remco. Using a round plastic sphere, you had to drop a metal ball from eight little cups, in order. They called it FRUSTRATION BALL because IRRITATING BALL was already taken.
$20

SHINDIG
Remco 1965
Among the first licensed games by Remco, along with HEIDI ELEVATOR and HULLABALOO. Based on the ABC TV show starring Jimmy O'Neill, it was basically a simple music trivia game.
$45 - $55

Inside of SHINDIG.

HEIDI ELEVATOR GAME
Remco 1965
"Based on the Heidi Pocketbook Doll, as seen on TV," which was, of course, made by Remco. This simple game, more in the traditional game style (with pawns and spinner), involves players riding up and down an elevator, waiting for the proper time to get on or off a floor (kind of like DONKEY KONG JR.) and reach the bottom. If two Heidi's occupy the same floor at the same time, they must shout "Hi, Heidi" or lose a turn (really).
$55 - $65

Inside of HEIDI ELEVATOR GAME.

FAMILY AFFAIR
Remco 1968
Based on the CBS TV series starring Brian Keith. All the games from this period have simplistic line art on the insert and board. Depending on which section of the board the player is on, the dice will have different meaning. If you're on the Bus and roll a three, Buffy forgot Mrs. Beasley, so you must go back to the Zoo. Roll a one in the Park and you lose a turn. Player who manages to get all five family members back home wins.
$150 - $200

LOST IN SPACE 3D ACTION FUN GAME
Remco 1966
(Exists in color.) Based on the CBS TV series starring the "Space Family Robinson." The most valuable game that Remco made is a simple track game that happens to have three levels. Plastic spacemen obey a spinner and leap from level to level amidst a cardboard futuristic background.
$450 - $550

CHITTY CHITTY BANG BANG ELECTRIC QUIZ GAME
Remco 1968
Based on the movie starring Dick Van Dyke. In 1968-69, Remco released a whole bunch of licensed board games, and all of them are highly prized. This one is similar to HULLABALOO and is essentially a movie trivia game.
$55 - $70

side of FAMILY AFFAIR.

JOURNEY TO THE UNKNOWN
Remco 1968
Based on the (short-lived)ABC TV series. Rare game in which players must visit secret rooms, collect cards and hurry back to safety. The problem is you don't know where the cards you need are in the many rooms, so you must visit quite a few before collecting all three. A special dice could double your spin.
$250 - $300

HE MOD SQUAD
mco 1968
sed on the ABC TV series. The game is "As Timely as Today's Headlines," which esn't say a lot for it. Pretty much a game of CLUE, with players going to places on e board looking for clues. Groovy art on the inside, though.
75- $225

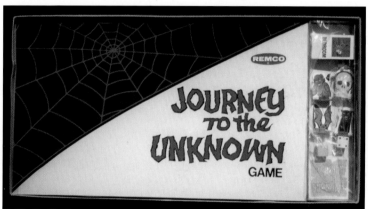

Inside of JOURNEY TO THE UNKNOWN.

HAWAII FIVE-O
Remco 1968
Based on the CBS TV series starring Jack Lord. Game involves Steve McGarrett and his associates searching for information about a crime at various locations on the board, like the Shopping District or the South Beach District.
From the collection of Michael Quinn
$250 - $300

ide of MOD SQUAD.

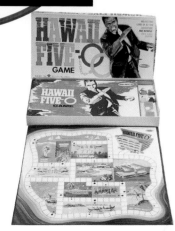

Inside of HAWAII FIVE-O.

LANCER
Remco 1969
Based on the CBS TV series.
Courtesy of Rick Polizzi
$100 - $125

MAGIC! MAGIC! MAGIC! GAME
Remco 1975
Remco recycled components of many magician toy packages into this game where players are forced to perform tricks successfully.
$25 - $30

Not Shown: **THAT GIRL,** Remco 1969, $250 - $350; **SPORTS ELECTRIC QUIZ** Remco 1969, $20 - $30; **MONKEY AUTO RACES,** Remco 1967, $25 - $35; and **COMBINATION DICE GAME** Remco 1960s(?), $100 - $150.

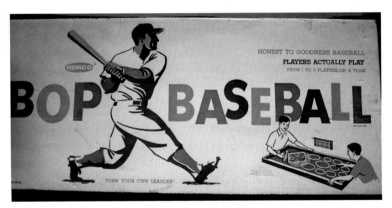

BOP BASEBALL
Remco 1961
HUGE wooden game (6 feet long!) had players actually using a bat to hit a baseball puck into scoring position on the board. Uncommon.
$50- $75

THE MYSTERY ZODIAC
Remco 1969
Large plastic device is more of a fortune telling machine than a game. Has logo which says "From the Little Old Toymaker."
$25 - $35

General games are those that defy easy categorization. To me, this section is the "Volkswagen" of board games, the "People's Games," "Meat and Potatoes" games. These are the games that have sustained the genre from the very beginning. These are the games that we grew up with, remember, and enjoy. While the "Porsches" of board games may get all the attention and corresponding value, the games with no special affiliation and no celebrity endorsement remain in our hearts. Collectors eagerly seek out CANDYLAND and MYSTERY DATE because they are fun and complete a link to our past. No one buys the HOGAN'S HEROES BLUFF OUT GAME for its play value.

Card games, marble games, skill and action games, educational games, and games of every description that have historically formed the foundation of board games in general are found in this section.

GIANT COOTIE
Schaper 1950s
$125 - $150

GIANT COOTIE
Schaper 1972
First reissue of 1950s
Giant Cootie. Only 2
were included. Rare.
$45 - $55

GIANT COOTIE
Schaper 1950s
This was the same game as regular Cootie, but the pieces were
huge! The box itself is two feet tall, and the Giant Cooties dwarf a
regular cootie (actually a Marx "Busy Bee" rip-off). They were so
big they had plugs in their bellies, and doubled as banks. They must
of have a hard time selling these, as this game is rare, and subsequent reissues of this exact product happened into the 1970s.

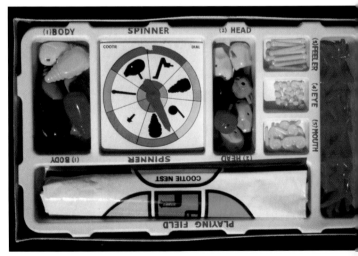

COOTIE HOUSE
Schaper 1966
Very rare game involving the use of Cooties, and a large plastic play mat.
$55 - $75

GIANT COOTIE
Schaper 1978
The last incarnation of the Giant Cootie. Even though the
Cootie style had officially changed, the original 1950s version was included in this set. Only two cooties were included.
$35 - $45

Inside of COOTIE HOUSE.

COOTIE
Schaper 1972
This is a few years after the classic
Cootie was re-styled. They claimed
the molds had worn out. (See first
book for other versions).
$20 - $25

BEETLE
Chad Valley 1960s
English game, a direct rip-off of
COOTIE, with the same pieces.
$20 - $25

BUG
Unknown 1960s
Small, Japanese rip-off of COO-
TIE.
Courtesy of Jeff Lowe's
ExtravaGAMEza
$10 - $20

SPACE BUG
Wm. Drueke and Sons, Inc. 1959
Very poor man's COOTIE, with plastic pegs covering
painted cootie picture on wooden blocks.
$10 - $15

SCARECROW
Schaper 1952
Early Schaper game,
same as DUNCE (see
first book).
$25 - $35

BUSY BEE
Marx 1950s
Canadian rip-off of COOTIE. It's obvious that copies were made of
the original Cootie, and cheesy wings were added to make "bees."
$25 - $30

MILL
Schaper 1950s
"Based on the old favorite."
Rather than a piece of wood and
golf tees, plastic men were used.
$20 - $25

MILL
Schaper 1960s
Reissue.
$10 - $15

SHIFTY GEAR
Schaper 1962
Try to connect your gears from one side of the board to the other.
$25 - $35

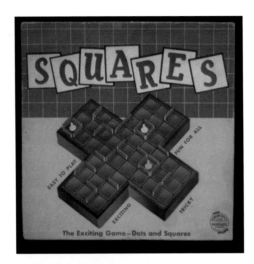

SQUARES
Schaper 1950s
Try to trap your opponent's "dot" with your "square."
$10 - $15

PUT AND TAKE
Schaper 1956
This simple game, involvin putting chips in and taking chips out, remained in the line for many years.
$10 - $12

TIDDLE-TAC-TOE
Schaper 1950s
Cross between Tiddley Winks and Tic-Tac-Toe.
$12 - $15

Right:
PUT AND TAKE
Schaper 1960s
Unusual cover art for them.
$20 - $25

Far Right:
GUESS' N BEE
Schaper 1960s
Obscure game. Guess the word and a jet of air reveals the missing letters. Guess wrong and you're "stung."
$30 - $40

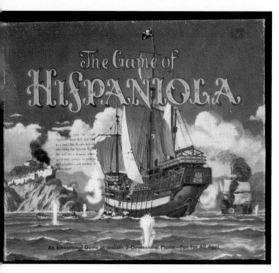

HISPANIOLA
Schaper 1957
Very unusual and *very* rare "historical" game for Schaper. Must have been made at the same time [as] TREASURE ISLAND. Beautiful cover.
$75 - $100

NIBBLES N' BITES
Schaper 1964
Magnetic switch on the ol' FISH POND game.
$30 - $40

Inside of HISPANIOLA.

DUNCE
Schaper 1960s
Photo cover version (see first book for other editions).
$20 - $25

DON'T SPILL THE BEANS
Schaper 1967
Actually uses real dried beans. I think it's the only game to use an actual food product.
$20 - $25

JACK AND THE BEANSTALK
Schaper 1965
Cool game had players gathering plastic leaves of giant stalk and climbing to the top. First one there made giant pop out of castle (and he presumably ate you).
$35 - $40

KING OF THE HILL
Schaper 1968
"Hazards, Pitfalls, Obstacles, Traps Galore." First one to the top made plastic "Crown" pop out. Photo cover.
$20 - $25

TICKLE BEE
Schaper 1956
Second biggest seller behind COOTIE. Magnetic game.
$35 - $40

Right:
KING OF THE HILL
Schaper 1950s
$25 - $30

Below:
HORSE PLAY
Schaper 1962
Standard horse race game given Schaper treatment.
$45 - $55

TICKLE BEE
Schaper 1976
Sellers sometimes (unknowingly) misrepresent this game. The only copyright says 1956, but actually the box is smaller, and the board graphics are different from the expensive 1956 version. The dead giveaway is the "new" cootie logo in the upper right corner of the box, which didn't start being used until 1969.
$15 - $20

Left:
PUCK-LUCK HOCKEY
Schaper 1960s
Scarce magnetic game similar to TICKLE BEE.
$40 - $45

Right:
SHAKE-A-LEG
Schaper 1971
Unique timer used a marble and centrifugal force.
$15 - $20

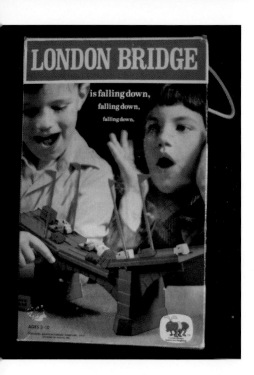

LONDON BRIDGE
Schaper 1972
Schaper changed the
box style of their
games in the late
1960s. Their boxes
became more like
carrying cases and
had a built in string
"handle."
$15 - $20

HUMPTY DUMPTY
Schaper 1971
Simplistic game. Some
people only collect the
plastic Humpty Dumpty
figure.
$20 - $30

HAVE-A-HEART
Schaper 1960s
Here's a horrifying game in which opponents try to "dislodge
clip-on hearts" with the enclosed plastic swords.
$25 - $35

CASPER THE FRIENDLY GHOST
Schaper 1974
$35 - $40

SOMBRERO
Schaper 1971
Players try to get their marbles
through a maze and into the
center of a precariously balanced sombrero.
$20 - $25

CASPER THE FRIENDLY GHOST
Schaper 1974
Neat game in which all pieces glowed in the dark, and Casper
himself lit up when placed in the correct configuration. I have
two of these games, and I have yet to figure out how to make
him light up. This game and I'M GEORGE GOBEL (Schaper
1955) are the only two games Schaper got a character license
for (see first book).

DON'T BREAK THE ICE
Schaper 1969
Classic game uses the plastic boy figure from DUNCE.
$10 - $15

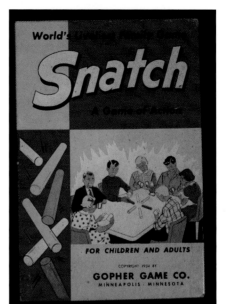

SNATCH
Gopher Game Co. 1954
There must be some connection between Schaper and this company (that made a lousy version of SPOONS). It uses the exact same size box, colors, and lettering as the 1950s COOTIE (see first book). Both companies are also from Minneapolis, Minnesota. Relation or rip-off?
$10 - $15

WING-IT
Schaper 1971
Shooting gallery.
$20 - $25

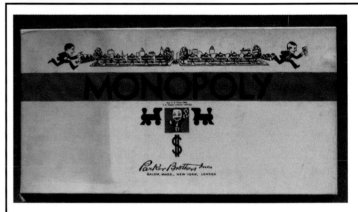

MONOPOLY
Parker Brothers 1936
White Box Number 9 Edition. Full box version with unusual tokens, like an old lantern, with a green celluloid shade (see first book).
$75 - $100

LIL SQUIRT
Smethport Speciality Co. 1950s
A low-rent rip-off cross between Schaper's SKUNK (see first book) and TICKLEBEE.
$10 - $15

MONOPOLY lantern playing piece.

MONOPOLY
John Waddington Ltd. 1960s
British version had different property titles.
$25 - $35

TIPPY TEEPEE
Schaper 1970
The game of JACK STRAWS.
$20 - $25

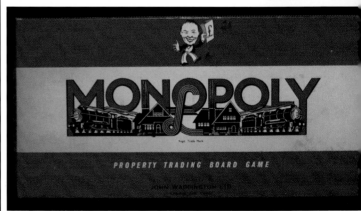

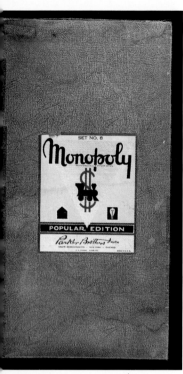

MONOPOLY
Parker Brothers 1980s
German Version.
$20 - $30

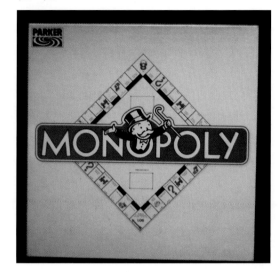

MONOPOLY
Spiele-Schmidt 1960s
German. Unusual square box had board
folded up into quarters.
$35 - $45

MONOPOLY
Parker Brothers 1951
Popular Edition, Set Number Eight. Rare full
box version. Had Grand Hotels and
"cobbled" playing board.
$100 - $150

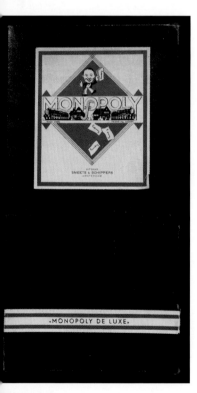

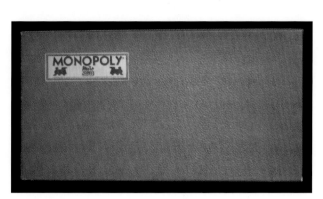

MONOPOLY
Parker Brothers/MIRO 1960s
French version.
$20 - $30

STOCK EXCHANGE
Chessex 1992
Reproduction of original rare Monopoly
expansion set (see first book). You put
this set on "Free Parking," and you
have additional fun with your game.
$25 - $35

MONOPOLY
Smeets & Schippers 1960s
De Luxe German version. Houses and hotels
are wedge-shaped.
$30 - $40

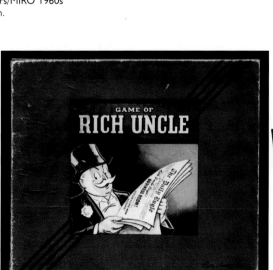

RICH UNCLE
Parker Brothers 1950s
Spin-off of MONOPOLY.
Variant (see first book).
$40 - $50

RICH UNCLE
Parker Brothers
1946
$55 - $65

RICH UNCLE
Parker Brothers
1965
$25 - $35

OLD MAID
All-Fair 1940s
"With Characters from Famous Nursery Rhymes and Fairy Tales." The characters make this edition valuable.
$30 - $40

OLD MAID
Whitman 1960s
This very tiny set of cards is popular among collectors.
$20 - $25

FLINCH
Parker Brothers 1954
One of endless versions (see first book).
$10 - $15

CLUEDO
Waddington 1965
Although this is a newer version, this is the game that our CLUE (see first book) comes from.
From the collection of Bob Claster
$25 - $35

OLD MAID
Parker Brothers 1950s
The old favorite.
$10 - $12

ROOK
Parker Brothers 1943
This version stills credits the Rook Card Co., whom Parker Brothers originally had make the game (see first book).
$15 - $20

SPOOF
Milton Bradley 1918
Originally advertised
as a war-like strategy
game.
$20 - $25

CROW
Parker Brothers 1959
Canadian version. Rare car travel game.
$20 - $25

QUICK WIT
Parker Brothers 1938
Gluyas Williams cover
as value (see first
book).
10

PLAZA
Parker Brothers 1913
obscure card game.
0 - $15

KAPU
Polynesian Cards, Inc. 1958
"KAPU is the Picture Story card
game of Hawaii."
$8 - $10

DOUBLE SOME 'R' SET
Parker Brothers 1947
"And some are not."
From the collection of Bob Claster
$7 - $10

BUNCO
Home Game Co. 1904
"The game of the year."
$15 - $25

OH HELL
Cadaco 1973
"Like the old favorite but a H...
of a lot more fun."
From the collection of Bob Claster
$15 - $20

CANASTA
Unknown 1950s?
Simple set of cards and rules.
$5

MOVIE TRIVIA GAME
Hoyle 1984
"Series One." Trivia cards.
$5

NEVADA
V.M. Hayes 1950s
Promotional game from casinos.
$15 - $20

NEVADA BLACKJACK
E.S. Lowe 1960s
"Includes Painted Cloth Layout."
$10

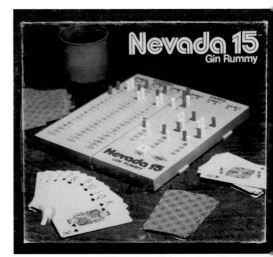

**NEVADA 15
GIN RUMMY**
E.S. Lowe 1975
$7 - $10

MICHIGAN RUMMY
Transogram 1969
14" playing tray.
$5

STRATEGY POKER
Milton Bradley 1967
"Fine Edition." Others in the series included
BACKGAMMON, RUMMY, etc.
$15 - $20

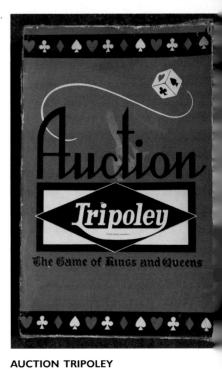

AUCTION TRIPOLEY
Cadaco-Ellis 1940
Rare. There are many versions of the card game
TRIPOLEY (see first book).
$15 - $20

TRIPOLEY
Cadaco-Ellis 1948
"Club Edition."
$10 - $15

HEARTS
Parker Brothers 1914
"An Exciting Letter Game." Dice, too.
$10 - $15

GO GIN
Ideal 1968
"Card word game." Unusual for Ideal.
$15 - $20

YAHTZEE
E.S. Lowe/Milton Bradley 1973
$7

CRIBBAGE
Hoyle 1960s
"Official." Cherry Wood board.
$5

TRIPLE YAHTZEE
E.S. Lowe 1972
$10 - $15

KISMET
Spare-Time Corp.
1943
Not the dice game.
Similar to TRIPOLEY.
Sexy cover.
$25 - $30

TRIPLE YAHTZEE
Milton Bradley 1982
$5

WORD YAHTZEE
Milton Bradley 1982
Now you roll the
dice for letters
instead of numbers.
$8 - $10

SPILL AND SPELL
Parker Brothers 1960s
The first WORD YAHTZEE.
$10 - $15

SPLIT WORDS
Holiday Games 1963
Or maybe this is the first
SPILL AND SPELL.
$12

ELECTRO-DICE
Radio Shack 1960s
Electronic flashing dice, for those of us
too lazy to throw the die.
$10 - $15

SCRABBLE
Selchow & Righter 1953
One of the top ten most popular games of all time. This
version was still being made for the Production and Marketing Company, for whom Selchow & Righter made the game.
$20 - $25

SCRABBLE
Selchow & Righter 1953
Curious "Magnetic" version. Might have been home-made job, but I don't think so.
Board has metal under graphics, and pieces have magnet squares glued to them.
$25 - $35

TRAVEL SCRABBLE
Selchow & Righter 1953
"Number 53." Small, very
unusual travel edition.
Plastic board and small
word pegs.
$55- $75

BALI
Selchow & Righter 1954
Obscure card game made by the makers of SCRABBLE.
$20 - $25

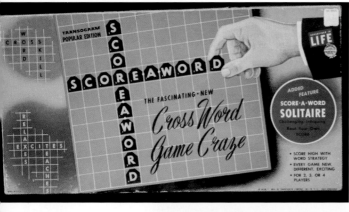

SCORE-A-WORD
Transogram 1953
"Popular Edition." Yet another
SCRABBLE rip-off (see first book).
$10 - $15

THIRTEEN
Cadaco-Ellis 1955
Exactly like SCRABBLE, but with numbers. One of the
boys on the cover wears Hopalong Cassidy slippers.
$15 - $20

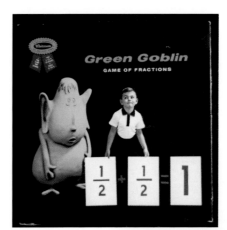

GREEN GOBLIN
Whitman 1962
"Game of Fractions." Isn't that a
contradiction? This series
included HAPPY LANDING,
and probably more.
$15 - $20

Right:
HAPPY LANDING
Whitman 1962
"A Geography Game."
$15 - $20

WATCH WORD
Ideal 1966
Wind up word game. Mecha-
nism similar to HANDS
DOWN (see first book).
$20 - $25

PLAY ON WORDS
E.S. Lowe 1971
From a rare series that
included NUMBERS UP
and SHOWDOWN
POKER (see first book).
*Courtesy of Jeff Lowe's
ExtravaGAMEza*
$12 - $15

NUMBERS UP
E.S. Lowe 1971
Courtesy of Jeff Lowe's ExtravaGAMEza
$12 - $15

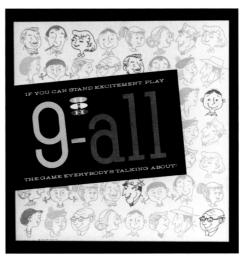

9 -ALL
Happy Hour 1956
"If you can stand excite-
ment, play...."
$15 - $20

TUF
Tuf, Inc. 1967
Another numbers game.
$10 - $12

FOCUS
Whitman 1960s
From the collection of Bob Claster
$15 - $20

**BACKGAMMON-PARCHEESI
COMBINATION**
Selchow & Righter 1930
Very scarce combo set (before
Scrabble, Parcheesi was Selchow &
Righter's bread and butter).
$35 - $45

CHEQUERO
Co-5 1960s
From the makers of AGGRAVATION (see first book).
$15 - $20

WORDCROSS
Intellect Games 1975
From a series of games called "Brief Encounter Games" that included SPECTRUM, QUITS, EGGHEAD, and CYPHER.
Courtesy of Jeff Lowe's ExtravaGAMEza
$10 - $12

COMBINATION GAME SET
...sa Games 1950s
...n example of the combination games sets that were common in the 1950s.
...ney often came in briefcases like this, and had all kinds of games.
...0 - $75

TROKE
Selchow & Righter 1961
Castle Checkers.
$20

CONQUEROR CHESS
...asantime Games 1962
...at chess set.
...5 - $35

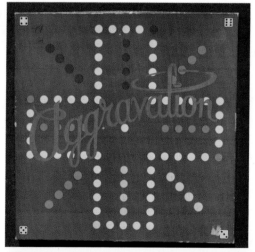

AGGRAVATION
Co-5 1962
The *real* no-fooling original edition of this game (see first book).
$10 - $15

Below:
AGGRAVATION
Co-5 1960s
"Deluxe Party Edition."
$10 - $15

PARK AND SHOP
...6 TO ADULT   PRICE $3.00
...nation's hustle-bustle traffic game sen-
...on. The object is to outsmart the other
...ers by parking your car in a strategic
...e, completing your shopping quickly
...being the first to return home.
...'s lots of fun for 2 to 6 players.

DISSECTED U.S.-WORLD MAP
AGES 7 TO 12   PRICE $1.50, OTHER $1.00
Interesting and educational, the colorful
Tekwood U.S. map is cut on state lines
and lists state capitals, historic places,
common products and manufactured items.
Reverse side pictures a map of the world.
Completed size of the map is 14" x 20".

WORD"WISE"
...TO ADULT   PRICE $2.00
...scinating word game played with
...s plus a unique "Word Pun" fea-
...found in no other game. Packed
...fun, strategy and skill as you build
...on strategic scoring squares. Keen
...etition for 2, 3, or 4 players.

BIG BEN JIG SAW PUZZLE
AGES 10 TO ADULT   PRICE $1.00
Big Ben puzzles are the grand-daddies of
all puzzles. There are 12 different puzzles,
each with 1000 interlocking pieces. Each
one faithfully reproduces a famous painting in all its brilliant colors. Completed
puzzle size is 20" x 28", card table size.

RACK-O
Milton Bradley 1956
Original edition of this fun game (see first book).
$15 - $22

QUBIC
Parker Brothers 19?
3-D Tic Tac Toe.
$7 - $10

GIANT DOUBLE HI-Q
Kohner 1960s
Large version of small game.
$20 - $25

SORRY!
Parker Brothers 1934
(Shown without board). "The Fashionable English Game."
Like CLUE, Sorry originally came from England (see first book).
$30 - $40

PARCHEESI
Selchow & Righter 1975
Unusual 100th Anniversary version.
$15 - $25

MAH-JONGG
Parker Brothers 1923
Selling for the Mah-Jon Sales Co. of America, a the height of the craze (see first book).
$50 - $60

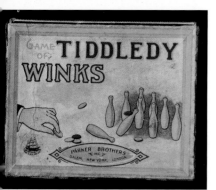

TIDDLEDY WINKS
Parker Brothers 1900s?
Different games could be played, with winks and small bowling pins. Came with glass cup, which is of special interest to some collectors.
$25 - $35

BATS IN YOUR BELFRY
Mattel 1964
A timer popped plastic bats up out of a castle. Players had to catch them with giant, webbed Creature-from-the-Black-Lagoon hands.
$55 - $75

Below:
HAUNTED HOUSE
Ideal 1962
Another cool, giant game. Players move through what amounts to a 3-D board, opening hidden doors while listening to the "hooting owl" spinner, and searching for the hidden jewel in the attic. Great box graphics.
$350 - $450

AMPIRE MONSTER GAME
keside 1970s
5 - $35

EREWOLF MONSTER GAME
keside 1970s
5 - $45

ONSTROUS MONSTER GAME
keside 1970s
5 - $45

ORD GAME OF GHOST
keside 1970s
0 - $25

ese scary games (a series by Lakeside) were all dice
mes in plastic figural containers, like Soakies.
four games courtesy of Rick Polizzi

ONSTER LAB
al 1964
is huge game is every collector's dream. Players fight to keep a
torized monster from coming to their side. When he reaches the
, his mask pops off, revealing a hideous skeletal face. Neat!
0 - $500

Inside HAUNTED HOUSE.

YIPES!
Ideal 1976
TROUBLE, with
monsters.
$10 $15

COUNT DOWN
Transogram 1960
Beautiful space game.
Courtesy of Rick Polizzi
$40 - $50

STEVE SCOTT SPACE SCOUT
Transogram 1952
Early space game. Game named after Transogram's
President's grandson. How's *that* for an ego-boost?
$75 - $100

ORBIT
Parker Brothers 1966
Reissue of 1959 game with new graphics.
From the collection of Bob Claster
$20 - $25

LUNAR LANDING
Lay's 1969
For some reason, the Lay's Potato Chips people made a space game involving the
Big, Bad Wolf and the Three Little Pigs. Game keeps being offered for sale in
mint, unpunched condition, suggesting a warehouse find.
$30 - $40

SWOOP
Whitman 1969
Kind of a space version of SORRY.
$15 - $20

EARTH SATELLITE
Gabriel 1956
Very rare.
Courtesy of Jeff Lowe's ExtravaGAMEza
$75 - $125

SPACE WALK
Selchow & Righter 1970
Skill game maneuvering a
marble through a tilting
maze, kind of like SOM-
BRERO.
$30 - $40

ASTRO LAUNCH
Ohio Art 1963
Scarce game by this company. Metal
board. Space version of TROUBLE.
$75 - $100

MOON FLIGHT
Avon 1970
$20 - $25

MOON FLIGHT
Avon 1970
Giant game board, moving pieces, instructions,
Apollo rocket with Moon lander, and an American
flag were all jammed into this neat game by Avon.
And when you were done, you could douse your-
self with the contents of the rocket. How many
games can you do *that* with?

...de of ASTRO LAUNCH.

MOUSE CAT SCRAMBLE
Steven Mfg. 1967
$15 - $20

CAT AND MOUSE
Parker Brothers 1964
Little plastic mice moved around the board, and tried not to fall into the cat's traps.
$15 - $20

MOUSE CAT SCRAMBLE
Steven Mfg. 1967
Small game similar to RED SKELTON'S "I DOOD IT," SCAT (see first book) and JACK BE NIMBLE. Players place their mice in the center of the table and hold them by their tails. When the "Cat" figure appears on the dice all players must yank their mice as fast as they can, while the cat must attempt to trap the mice with the plastic cat. In this case, when the cat slams down, it makes a "squeak" noise from the built in squeaker. Lots of neat graphics.

CATCH 'EM
Mattel 1969
Huge plastic cheese and magnetic mice.
$20 - $25

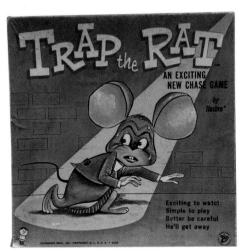

TRAP THE RAT
Hasbro 1964
Plastic fences try to surround an escaping rat. Some games came with a plastic mouse piece, others with a metal mouse.
$20 - $25

KING OF THE CHEESE
Milton Bradley 1959
Big cardboard cheese and sticky mice.
Courtesy of Jeff Lowe's ExtravaGAMEza
$35 - $45

3 BLIND MICE
Lakeside 1967
Game container was small
plastic piece of cheese.
$15 - $20

RECALL
Milton Bradley 1967
Players had to reconstruct a fast moving image from a pile of images.
$25 - $35

JACK BE NIMBLE
The Embossing Company 1940s?
Same game as MOUSE CAT SCRAMBLE.
$10 - $15

DON'T BUG ME
Hasbro 1967
"The game that will
drive you buggy."
Players attempt to fling
bugs through a small
opening in a net. First
one to get rid of his
bugs wins.
$20 - $25

CHARADES
Selchow & Righter 1968
Plain old charades, but with
timer and score pads.
$10 - $12

BIRD BRAIN
Milton Bradley 1966
Like the card game BINGO.
$25 - $35

CHERRY PIE
Transogram 1966
"Even tots can play." Same game as STAY ALIVE (see first book).
$20 - $25

ROTTEN EGG
Hasbro 1966
Players try to reassemble their
colored plastic eggs.
$20 - $25

Don't dress.

It's a pool party. It's a barbecue. A game-room get-together. You've been skiing, skating, to a ball game. The mood's informal. You're in slacks, shorts, bathing suits, ski pants. What's for fun? TWISTER. Play it indoors or out, with 2 players, 4 players or teams. TWISTER's the craziest game in a month of fundays. Teen-agers are wild about it. Kids can't stop playing it. And anyone who likes life lively will love it. And it's so simple you can explain it in a minute. TWISTER's a stocking-feet game, played on a mat, great fun to watch. TWISTER goes with sandwiches and do-it-yourself sundaes, with knockwurst and beer, with hamburgers and corn-on-the-cob. Serve everything buffet style, spin records, and pin a paper medal on the champion twister and give him a TWISTER game to take home.

FUNNY FINGER
Ideal 1968
I can imagine kids
breaking their digits
on this one.
$15 - $20

ANIMAL TWISTER
Milton Bradley 1967
For the kiddies.
$20 - $25

BARK N' BITE
Ideal 1969
Players try to avoid the dog as
they deliver the mail. Obscure
game.
$25 - $35

TOWER CLIMB
Milton Bradley 1971
Neat game in which you and a partner must work together
to raise a plastic ball up and out of the tower.
$15 - $20

TILTIN' MILTON
Ideal 1968
One of many plastic bal-
ancing games, like HUN-
GRY HENRY (see first
book).
$20 - $25

72

HURRY WAITER!
Ideal 1967
$25 - $35

HOT DIGGITY DOG
Transogram 1967
"The Amusement Park Fun Game." The plastic hot dog machine determined your moves. Plastic weiners!
$25 - $35

HURRY WAITER!
Ideal 1967
large, nerve-wracking game in which one player must memorize what other players have ordered, and then quickly bring their orders to them while balancing a revolving timer-tray. The good news is there is lots of plastic fruit.

GIGGLE POOL
Unknown 1950s?
I'm not sure why it was called Giggle or Pool, because you do neither. Basically you're using bellows to blow a Styrofoam ball into your opponents corner.
$20

SANDLOT SLUGGER
Milton Bradley 1968
"Slugging Sam," the mechanical batter, was spring loaded and basically played Tee-Ball in this popular action game.
$25 - $35

SCARECROW
Ideal 1975
Shoot the giant plastic scarecrow in the proper spot and he'll fall to pieces.
$55 - $75

LEAP FROG
Lakeside 1966
"Skill-Toss Action Game." You toss
rubber frogs at plastic lily pads for
points.
$35 - $45

BANDERSNATCH
Mattel 1968
The game of COOTIE, only you're
building a Bandersnatch.
$30 - $35

MR. MAD
Ideal 1970
Super cool game in
which a battery-operated
robot spins out of con-
trol, spewing marbles, if
you put the wrong
marble in the wrong
spot.
$35 - $45

MR. REMBRANDT
Ideal 1970
Kind of a motorized Spirograph.
$30 - $40

Left:
Inside of MR. MAD.

SMACK-A-ROO
Mattel 1964
"Play Baseball, Bowling, Smack-it, and Many
Other Wonderful Games."
$25 - $35

TU TU
Ideal 1963
"The Tossin' Turtle." Large plastic turtle plays catch with you, providing you throw the ball exactly in his mouth.
$30 -$40

FANG BANG
Milton Bradley 1967
Bizarre game in which players don witch doctor masks and try to beat each other with balloon snakes until they burst.
$30 - $40

BOP THE BEETLE
Ideal 1962
Basically Tiddely Winks, with large plastic beetles that you try to "bop" into the giant frog's mouth.
$65 - $75

CAREFUL
Ideal 1967
"The toppling tower game." Nerve-wracking game in which players take turns removing parts of a tower indicated by the spinner.
$25 - $35

BABYSITTER
Ideal 1966
Large, scarce game in which the object is not to wake up the spring loaded baby while doing things that baby-sitters do best, like listening to the radio, playing records and eating from the fridge. The baby makes a cute squeaking noise when he wakes up.
$75 - $100

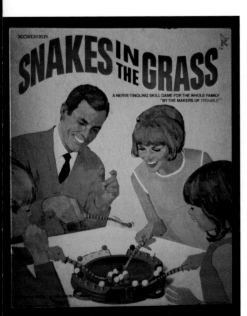

SNAKES IN THE GRASS
Kohner 1960
Players use wiggley rubber snakes to pick up colored marbles from a pit. Very irritating.
$25 - $35

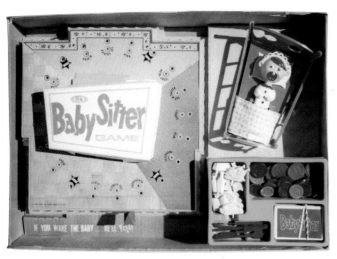

Inside of BABY-SITTER.

MONKEY SHINES
E.S. Lowe 1960s
Huge plastic palm tree is climbed by players' monkeys before the chimpanzee catches them. Is it just me, or do these kids have a lot of mascara on?
$20 - $25

MONKEY'S UNCLE
Transogram 1967
$40 - $50

CAGEY MONKEY
Whitman 1960s
Courtesy of Jeff Lowe's ExtravaGAMEza
$15 - $20

OPEN SESAME
Ideal 1972
Large, cool plastic "mountain" houses fabulous jewels. If you drop your marble at the right time, "open sesame," the door opens and the jewels are yours.
$20 - $25

MONKEY'S UNCLE
Transogram 1967
"A Stunt Festival," and no truer words were ever spoken. Gigantic game had tons of stunts that players had to rush to and perform, from fishing in a cardboard box to making sounds like a Monkey's Uncle. When the large Monkey Timer's eyes came full circle, the round was over. Scarce.

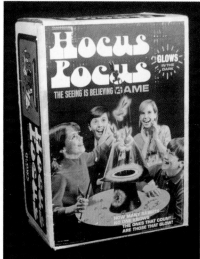

HOCUS POCUS
Transogram 1968
Glow in the dark rabbits
jump out of a hat. From a
"Glow" series that included
GREEN GHOST and KA-
BALA (see first book).
Courtesy of Rick Polizzi
$40 - $60

KOOKIE CHICKS
Milton Bradley 1967
Magnetic wands under the board con-
trolled these wacky Styrofoam eggs.
$20 - $25

WHERE'S WILLIE?
Milton Bradley 1966
Based on a stunt from *Shenanigans* TV show. Large game.
$30 - $40

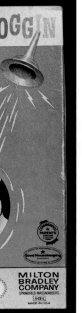

BOGGIN NOGGIN
Milton Bradley 1964
Stunt from *Shenanigans* TV show.
$15 - $20

SCOOT!
Transogram 1955
3-D game "House" board changed depending
on whether Mom or the Kids were home.
$12 - $15

HAPPY FACE
Milton Bradley 1968
Youngsters matched cards
to faces.
$10 - $15

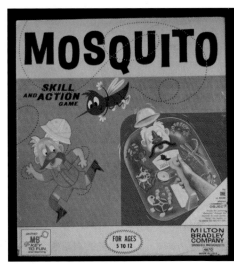

MOSQUITO
Milton Bradley 1966
Players tried to maneuver a spinning top for
points.
$30 - $40

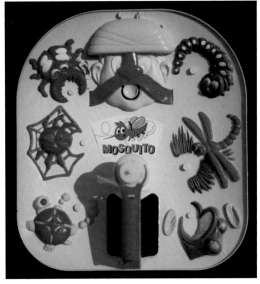

Inside of MOSQUITO.

BUG BOPPER
Magic Wand Corp. 1969
"Bop the bugs with the bug
bopper." Magnetic action game.
$10 - $15

TUMBLE BUMBLE
Ideal 1970
Large plastic capsules slide
down ramps into holes on the
board.
$20 - $30

Right:
FIRE HOUSE MOUSE
Transogram 1967
Players try to pull the cards
they need before the mouse
comes bobbing down the fire
pole. Transogram also used
this same concept for SPY'S-
A-POPPIN.
$30 - $40

Left:
GNIP GNOP
Parker Brothers 1971
I guess everyone knows by
now that GNIP GNOP is
PING PONG spelled back-
wards.
$15 - $20

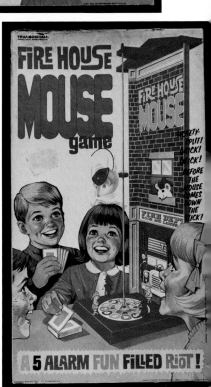

THREE KEYS TO TREA-SURE
Marx 1960
$75 - $100

RUBIK'S CUBE
Ideal 1980
"The Original" Rubik's Cube. Puzzle.
$15 - $20

TWIDDLER
Parker Brothers 1969
Maze game.
$10 - $15

THREE KEYS TO TREASURE
Marx 1960
Very large "Bagatelle" game in which players must try to line up the balls in three different sections on the board. When this is done, the locking mechanism is released and the treasure door pops open, revealing the prize that the wheel has turned to for that session. Marx did a lot of pinball machines and bagatelles, but this one is unique.

TIME BOMB
Milton Bradley 1964
Basically hot potato. Bomb goes off in hands of last one holding it. Great collector interest.
Courtesy of Rick Polizzi
$45 - $55

PLUG-A-JUG
Parker Brothers 1969
Word game in plastic jug container.
$7 - $10

BARREL OF MON-KEYS
Lakeside 1965
This original edition of the old favorite came in a cardboard container. Subsequent edition were in plastic barrels.
$30 - $40

GIGGLE STICK
Art Emboss Print Co.
1930s?
Players picked a stick and read the hilarious story.
$5 - $10

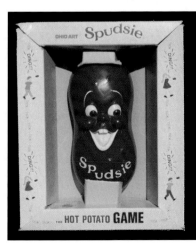

SPUDSIE
Ohio Art 1960s
"The Hot Potato Game." Same as TIME BOMB. Another rare Ohio Art game.
$30 - $40

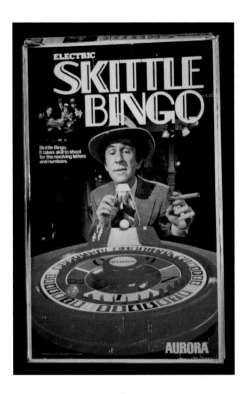

Left:
SKITTLE BINGO
Aurora 1973
Don Adams again appeared on the cover of this revolving electric bingo game.
$35 - $45

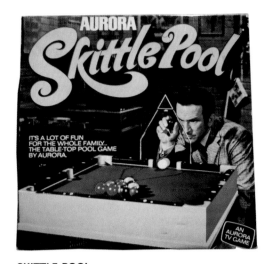

SKITTLE POOL
Aurora 1972
Don Adams appeared on the cover of this and the many other "Skittle" games that the original SKITTLE BOWL spawned, like SKITTLE HORSE SHOES, SKITTLE POKER, SKITTLE SHOOT-OUT, SKITTLE TIC-TAC-TOE, SKITTLE BINGO, and ALL-AMERICAN SKITTLE SCORE-BALL.
$50 - $65

HIGH STAKES
Hasbro 1973
Huge Vegas-style game featured Jerry Lewis on the cover. Others in this series included SPELLBOUND.
$30 - $40

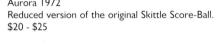

ALL AMERICAN SKITTLE SCORE-BALL
Aurora 1972
Reduced version of the original Skittle Score-Ball.
$20 - $25

SPELLBOUND
Hasbro 1973
Huge spelling game with Jerry Lewis on the cover.
$30 - $40

WHOOOPS
Aurora 1968
Interesting game that had kids balancing on small plastic bowls. How many broken ankles occurred? Box of rare game is same size and shape as Aurora's Monster Models of the period.
$20 - $30

TIGHT SQUEEZE
Mattel 1967
[M]others of America must have loved this game that had
[te]enagers joined at the groin with tight fitting plastic belts.
[$2]0 - $40

AIR TRIX
Milton Bradley 1976
"The Airstream Game." Super cool game involves moving a ball through
all kinds of obstacles while balancing it on a cushion of air.
$25 - $35

[B]OOB TUBE RACE
[Mil]ton Bradley 1962
[Th]is originally was a stunt from the
[Sh]enanigans TV show.
[$2]0 - $25

WHIRL OUT
Milton Bradley 1971
If you don't place your marbles carefully, the delicately balanced wheel will turn, spilling all your marbles.
$20 - $25

[RE]BOUND
[Ide]al 1971
[Shu]ffleboard, only rebounding off of corners.
[$1]5 - $20

PITCH-A-ROO
Milton Bradley 1975
Bean bag toss game.
$20

KNOCK-OFF!
Kenner 1969
Rare motorized game involves trying to keep the weird looking creature (Big Bopper) away from your side of the board where he'd knock off your playing piece (Fall Guy). Kind of like MONSTER LAB.
$35 - $45

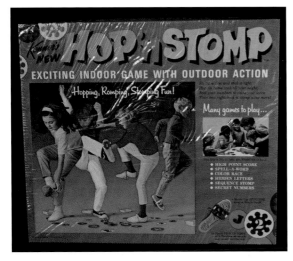

HOP 'N STOMP
Kenner 1969
No, those kids aren't doing the Ubangi Stomp; they're trying to pick up numbered discs with suction-cupped devices attached to their shoes.
$25 - $35

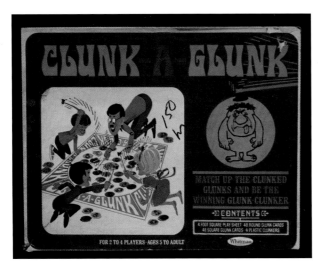

CLUNK-A-GLUNK
Whitman 1968
Another unfortunately named game involving players swinging suction-cupped hammers to grab clunks and glunks.
$30

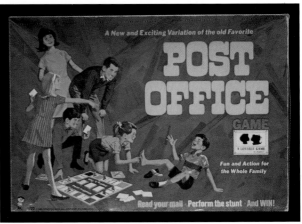

POST OFFICE
Hasbro 1968
"Read your mail - Perform the stunt." From a series of "Lovable Games" that included SPIN THE BOTTLE and THE GAME OF LOVE (see first book).
$25 - $35

BARNSTORMER
Marx 1970
The windup plane flies around the board, and no one knows who's pile of discs it will hit. Jack Davis illustration on instructions.
$20 - $25

PANIC!
Ideal 1965
Don't press the wrong button...
$25 - $35

SPRING CHICKEN
Mattel 1968
Putting a feather in the wrong place could cause you to lose all your marbles.
$20 - $25

ROCK PAPER SCISSORS
Ideal 1968
...they could make CHARADES into a board game, ...ey could make this into one too.
25 - $35

MUSINGO
Mattel 1962
Musical Bingo. The "organ grinder" actually plays music, as in "Jack in the Box" technology.
$25 - $35

FINGER DINGER MAN
...attel 1969
...arce game, in unusual box.
...0 - $40

BIG THUMB
...attel 1970
...he player wears a giant oversized thumb and tries to steal chips, while all the other ...ayers try to smash his thumb with plastic hammers. Charming game.
...0 - $40

HAPPY, HAPPY BIRTHDAY
Mattel 1963
"You can tell it's Mattel, it sounds swell." A huge plastic birthday cake contained a "Jack in the Box" mechanism that popped open your "surprise" at the end of the song.
$35 - $45

HAPPY BIRTHDAY SURPRISE
Milton Bradley 1957
From a "square box" series of games that included
BUMPY, STOP, WONDERLAND, MIGHTY MOUSE,
MERRY CIRCUS, and JALOPY RACE.
$20 - $25

BRIDG-IT
Hasbro 1960
Players tried to place plastic pieces from one side of the
board to the other without the opponent blocking.
From the collection of Bob Claster
$15 - $20

BRIDG-IT
Hasbro 1961
Advanced Deluxe Edition. Rare.
$40 - $50

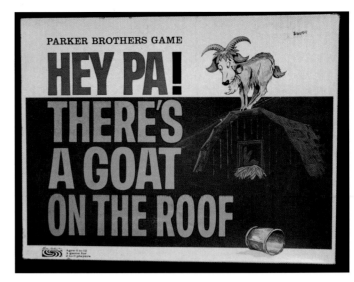

HEY PA! THERE'S A GOAT ON THE ROOF
Parker Brothers 1965
Favorite with collectors despite (or perhaps because of) the stupid title. 3-D
board had players trying to get from point A to point B without encountering
the goat. A little bell summoned the farmer.
$35 - $45

SPEEDWAY
Ideal 1961
As in a carnival, you smacked the bottom of this device to send the ball
soaring up the board. From a "Big Bopper" series that included SKIN DIVER.
$40 - $45

FINDER'S KEEPERS
Milton Bradley 1968
"The Thinking Game Where Memory Pays!"
$15 - $20

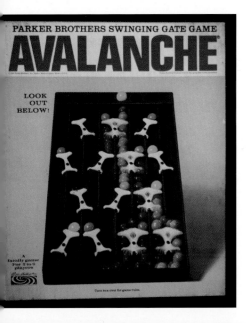

AVALANCHE
Parker Brothers 1966
Swinging gate marble game.
$20 - $25

KOO KOO CHOO CHOO
Ohio Art 1967
$55 - $75

OOT! TOOT!
elchow & Righter 1964
uper cool game has small wooden trains that move around the board.
40 - $55

KOO KOO CHOO CHOO
Ohio Art 1967
Very large and very heavy, elaborate rare game from Ohio Art, designed by Marvin Glass. It's kind of like TIME BOMB on wheels, or the movie SPEED. The Koo Koo Choo Choo can't stop, and it's carrying a load of Dynamite with a ticking timer. The object is to switch the tracks so that when it *does* explode, it does so on another player, and not you. Rare game.

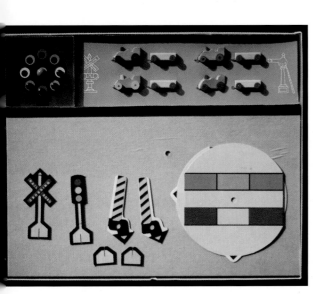

side of TOOT! TOOT!

DON'T DUMP THE DAISY
Ideal 1970
Plastic daisy is balanced on a stiff spring. Put the marbles on the wrong petal, and wham! Marbles all over the place.
$17 - $25

SLIPP' RY SPOONS
Ideal 1970
"Spin the top, get 3-in-a-row, Grab a spoon to win the show!"
$15 - $20

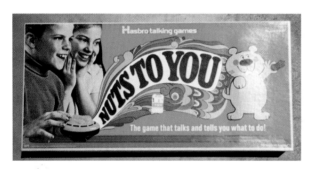

NUTS TO YOU
Hasbro 1969
Super cool game that has a plastic device that slides along a plastic strip. The device will speak different phrases, depending on where on the strip it is placed. Others in this series included GET IN THAT TUB, and HEY, FATSO.
Courtesy of Jeff Lowe's ExtravaGAMEza
$30 - $40

GET IN THAT TUB
Hasbro 1969
$30 - $40

HEY, FATSO
Hasbro 1969
Courtesy of Jeff Lowe's ExtravaGAMEza
$30 - $40

SENIOR ARTS PAINT BOX
AGES 6 TO 15   PRICE $4.00
Top quality art materials: 10 large and 12 medium wooden water color cups that won't come loose; 3 tubes of water colors; 16 Crayrite round crayons; 18 Crayrite No-Roll crayons; 3 jars of poster paint; water cup; brush; pictures and color chart.

GO TO THE HEAD OF THE CLASS
AGES 6 TO ADULT   PRICE $2.50
An educational and entertaining quiz game for juniors and adults with a classroom setting. Contains 792 questions and answers. Players advance from desk to desk, grade to grade, depending on knowledge, ingenuity, luck. Favorite for 2 to 8 players.

BINGO
AGES 6 TO ADULT   PRICE $1.00, OTHERS $.30-$2
A wonderful game for large group participation in the home or club room. This 50 card set includes 75 embossed wooden calling numbers, wooden markers, shaker box, tally sheets and directions. Also available in sets of 15, 25 and 100 cards.

EASY MONEY
AGES 6 TO ADULT   PRICE $2.50, OTHER $2.00
Lures youngsters and adults with its fast-moving spirit of chance and fortune. Build a real estate empire, run a night club, hotel, theatre, or conduct other businesses found in all walks of life. Here's 20,000 "dollars" in fun for 2 players or a crowd.

GO TO THE HEAD OF THE CLASS
Milton Bradley 1938
This is the 2nd Edition of this classic game, involving answering questions (see first book).
$30 - $45

LITTLE RED SCHOOL HOUSE
Parker Brothers 1952
This elaborate question and answer game seems to be in answer to Milton Bradley's GO TO THE HEAD OF THE CLASS.
$25 - $35

LUCKY BEE AND JOHNNY APPLESEED PRESCHOOL GAME BOX
Saalfield 1959
Simple games for the kiddies.
$10 - $15

JOHNNY *CAN* READ!
Ed-U-Cards 1956
"and Mary too!" Horrifying reading game in response to national debate in magazine articles about quality of schooling in America (Why Johnny Can't Read).
$10 - $15

OFF TO SCHOOL
Saalfield 1960
Has "OFF TO CAMP" game on opposite side, which explains the cover tag "Don't forget your books! Watch out for bears!"
$10 - $15

DIAL 'N SPELL
Milton Bradley 1961
Learn to spell.
$7 - $10

WHO DID IT?
Gardner Games 1950s
Obscure historical trivia game.
$15 - $20

MOTHER'S HELPER
Milton Bradley 1969
Game of helping Mother clean the house. Whoopee!
Courtesy of Jeff Lowe's ExtravaGAMEza
$12 - $18

LET'S FACE IT!
Hasbro 1955
$50 - $75

LET'S FACE IT!
Hasbro 1955
COOTIE game with Mr. Potato Head pieces. Players spin and, depending on which part of the anatomy the spinner points to, have to start building their figure. It's interesting to note that this game isn't called "The Mr. Potato Head Game," when it's obvious that's what it is. Two versions of the cover exist, with one proclaiming "As advertised in Life," and one without. Modestly described as the "Funniest Game in the World."

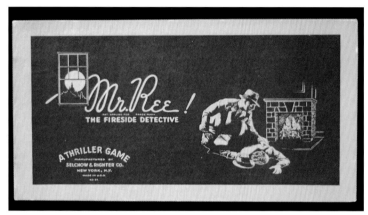

MR. REE!
Selchow & Righter 1937
Very rare version of this game (see first book) that has "composition" heads on the character cylinders. One of the forerunners of CLUE.
$125 - $150

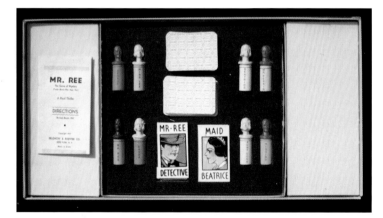

Inside of MR. REE!

FINGERS HARRY
Topper 1967
"Wildest, wackiest, most wonderful magnetic chase game yet." Fingers Harry or Patrolman Bill could "blow their top." Scarce game, one of a few this company made besides SILLY SAFARI (see first book).
$50 - $60

ESPIONAGE
Transogram 1963
Large, rare, elaborate spy game. From same series as DREAM DATE.
$75 - $100

Inside of ESPIONAGE.

SPY DETECTOR
Mattel 1963
Updated version of LIE DETECTOR (see first book). Scarce.
$45 - $55

WHODUNIT
Selchow & Righter 1973
Similar to CLUE.
$10

FLEA CIRCUS
Mattel 1964
Elaborate plastic magnetic game involving fleas.
$55 - $75

THE WINNING TICKET
Ideal 1977
"The great home lottery game." Designed by Sid Sackson.
From the collection of Bob Claster
$10 - $15

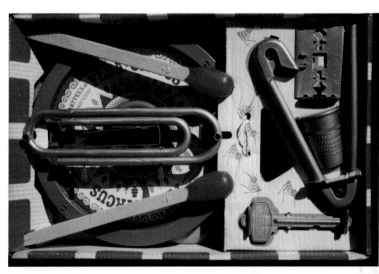

Inside of FLEA CIRCUS.

HAPPINESS
Milton Bradley 1972
Op-Art style game. Also known as THE GAME OF HAPPINESS (see first book).
$10 - $15

PIE FACE
Hasbro 1968
Russian Roulette with a spring loaded pie. It must have been a barrel of fun when that thing slammed into your face.
$45 - $55

Left:
PIVOT
Milton Bradley 1958
Kind of like BRIDG-IT.
$10

CLOCK-A-GAME
Topper 1966
Trivia against a large ticking timer. Games "reels" were changeable. The other game in the series was called CLOCK-A-WORD (see first book).
$35 - $45

TURTLE RACE
Ideal 1960s
A "Pillow Game." Clear inflatable pillow had games on both sides. Both were maze games, with Turtle Race having plastic turtles, and Mountain Climb using marbles. Scarce and Obscure. Not sure if there are others in the series.
$30 - $40

TEDDY BEAR PANDA
Parker Brothers 1940
"And his friends." Large, beautiful A B C animal game for the kiddies. Moving pieces actually have flocking on them to simulate fur. Tremendous.
$50 - $75

Inside of TEDDY BEAR PANDA.

UNNY RABBIT
rker Brothers 1950s
ute game had wooden carrots and cotton tails for Bunny playing pieces.
0 - $40

Right:
JALOPY RACE
Milton Bradley 1950s
$30 - $40

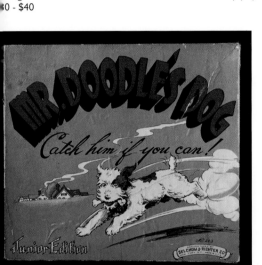

MR. DOODLE'S DOG
Selchow & Righter 1948
Rare, Junior Edition. Simplistic dog chase game created by Howard Garis, creator of Uncle Wiggley (see first book).
$40 - $45

BUMPY THE FUNNY LITTLE BEAR
Milton Bradley 1955
Instructions were on the side of these boxes, prompting many collectors to think they're missing.
$20 - $25

MERRY CIRCUS
Milton Bradley 1955
This later came out in a normal sized box.
$15 - $20

ONDER LAND
lton Bradley 1955
ays like CANDYLAND. Part of "Square Box" series that
cluded JALOPY RACE, BUMPY, MERRY CIRCUS,
GHTY MOUSE, and HAPPY BIRTHDAY SURPRISE.
5 - $35

NOAH'S ARK
Cadaco-Ellis 1945
$40 - $50

91

NOAH'S ARK
Cadaco-Ellis 1945
Like many Cadaco-Ellis games, large and colorful. Four players try to get two animals each of five different animals into the foldable cardboard ark. This game continued to be made by Cadaco into the 1970s, with the cardboard animals replaced with plastic ones.

HOPPITY
Parker Brothers 1961
"Help Hoppity hop through Happyland." Say that three times fast ... Neat game pieces are plastic kangaroos, with plastic baby kangaroos to go in their pouches. These pieces were originally made of wood.
$30 - $40

MICKEY MONK
Somerville 1930s
Simplistic Canadian track game, with golf theme.
Pair includes GAME OF FREDDIE FROG.
$30 - $40

Closeup of HOPPITY.

DON'T CATCH A COLD
Milton Bradley 1971
Elastic doo-dads kept the wobbling stinky cold bug out of your corner.
$20 - $30

FREDDIE FROG
Somerville 1930s
Courtesy of Jeff Lowe's ExtravaGAMEza
$30 - $40

ICE CUBE
Milton Bradley 1972
The mysterious game. Players make molds out of *real* ice, and go about the board trying not to melt, despite the danger of salt and hot washers. Many people had asked me about this game and, with the help of Tom Fassbender, I was able to figure out what the heck they were talking about. It seems to be a big hit with collectors, with no end to the outrageous prices being paid.
Courtesy of Uglytown Productions
$75 - $125

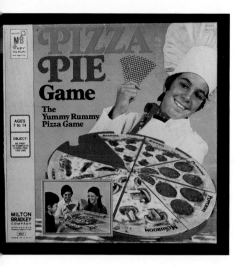

PIZZA PIE
Milton Bradley 1974
"The Yummy Rummy Pizza Game." The game of Rummy using cardboard pizza slices.
$20 - $25

BIRD WATCHER
Parker Brothers 1958
Beautiful game about ... you guessed it.
$25 - $35

ECTRIC COMIN' 'ROUND THE MOUNTAIN
ectric Game Co. 1954
other in Jim Prentice's "Electric" series which included
SEBALL, CHECKERS, BASKETBALL, HOLE IN THE
EAD, JACK STRAWS, FOOTBALL, and HOCKEY.
0 - $50

WUFFLE TREE
Selchow & Righter 1955
Simple kiddies game. From a series that included POW, BUZZ and WASH OUT.
$15 - $20

LLBILLIES COMIN' ROUND THE MOUNTAIN
sbro 1964
m a series that included HILLBILLIES HOEDOWN, and
LBILLIES FEUDIN' TIME. Supposedly the games were introduced to ride on the popularity of the *Beverly Hillbillies* TV show.
0 - $25

LUCKY CATCH
Whitman 1960s
FISH POND combined with a board game.
$5 - $10

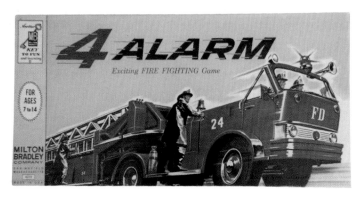

4 ALARM
Milton Bradley 1963
Game had little plastic fires.
Courtesy of Jeff Lowe's ExtravaGAMEza
$20 - $25

CLIMB THE MOUNTAIN
Parker Brothers 1951
CHUTES AND LADDERS on a mountain.
$25 - $35

REDDY-CLOWN 3-RING CIRCUS
Parker Brothers 1952
Large game with neat playing pieces.
$40 - $50

ICE CREAM
Gardner Games 1950s
Scarce game that included cardboard
money and cardboard ice cream.
$35 - $45

CORKY CLOWN
Hasbro 1964
"Big Top Circus Game
$15 - $20

CLOWN CAPERS
Whitman 1957
Simple child's game.
$10 - $12

KOOKY CARNIVAL
Milton Bradley 1969
Elaborate game with 9 different neat stunts. Two box covers exist (see first book).
$25 - $35

BODY ENGLISH
Milton Bradley 1967
Fine Edition. TWISTER with words.
$25 - $30

FUN HOUSE
Built-Rite 1950s
Like all Built-Rite games, of very little substance.
Courtesy of Jeff Lowe's ExtravaGAMEza
$10

DROP IN THE BUCKET
Milton Bradley 1968
New Fine Edition.
Game involves using paddles to pick up and place foam "ice cubes" into the bucket tied to the back of players. Unusual "ice bucket" game container.
$30 - $40

ONE MORE TIME
Milton Bradley 1967
Fine Edition. Dice game.
$15 - $20

LOLLI-POP LANE
Hasbro 1964
CANDYLAND wanna-be, with plastic lolli-pops given out to the winner.
$15 - $20

CANDYLAND
Milton Bradley 1949
This is the original version of this popular game, although it's not the one that most collector's remember (see first book).
$45 - $55

LOST TREASURE
Parker Brothers 1982
Neat electronic game of deep-sea diving. Uses logic to find treasure.
$25 - $35

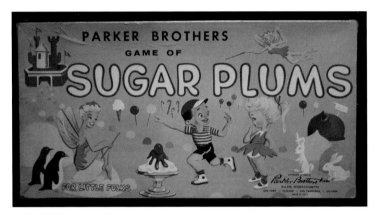

SUGAR PLUMS
Parker Brothers 1959
Another CANDYLAND-like game.
$20 - $25

Below:
DON'T MISS THE BOAT!
Parker Brothers 1965
$20 - $25

WHAT SHALL I BE?
Selchow & Righter 1969
Photo cover version of the 1966 popular girl's career game (see first book).
$25 - $35

WHAT SHALL I BE?
Selchow & Righter 1976
Edition Two. Attempts to correct the chauvinistic career choices of earlier editions by including Director, News Anchor, Astronaut, Lawyer, Doctor, and Jockey instead of Ballerina, Stewardess, Teacher, Beauty Queen, Actress, and Nurse.
$20 - $25

PLAY SAFE
Milton Bradley 1936
Bizarre game about children and safety, but it has cool metal "people" moving pieces.
$50 - $70

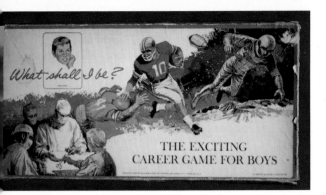

WHAT SHALL I BE?
Schow & Righter 1968
Boys Edition. Rare.
$30 - $40

I WISH I WERE
Milton Bradley 1964
$30 - $40

ESCORT
Parker Brothers 1955
"Game of Guys and Gals." Very odd artwork on this game
that is essentially Chinese Checkers. I guess the woman needs
an escort to protect her from all the marauding males.
$35 - $45

DREAM DATE
Transogram 1963
Large, elaborate magnetic game. "Use your personal
magnetism to 'click' with the boy of your choice." Same game workings as ESPIONAGE.
$35 - $45

I WISH I WERE
Milton Bradley 1964
"A game of pretending." Neat large plastic "board" and "dress-up dolls" combined
to make this obscure game interesting. Players moved around the board getting
the education or training they needed for their chosen career. First player to reach
the end becomes what they "wish they were." This game is years ahead of
Schow & Righter's WHAT SHALL I BE?, but has the same restrictions on careers
for girls: Models, Actress, Teacher, Stewardess, or Nurse.

SENIOR PROM
Built-Rite 1966
Warehouse find has reduced value.
$20 - $25

MONEY
Cadaco 1973
"Contains *Real Coins* from 10 different countries."
$15 - $20

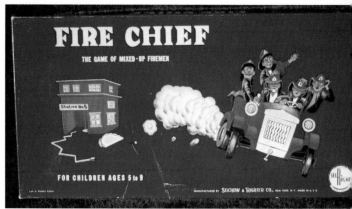

FIRE CHIEF
Selchow & Righter 1957
"The Game of Mixed-Up Firemen." The series included POSTMAN, MECHANIC MAC, POLICEMAN, and ENGINEER (see first book).
$15 - $20

SPOT CASH
Milton Bradley 1959
"A new type game of logic and skill."
$10 - $15

POLICEMAN
Selchow & Righter 1957
"The Game of Cops & Robber."
$25 - $30

MECHANIC MAC
Selchow & Righter 19?
"The Jolly Jalopy Game?
$20 - $25

THREE LITTLE PIGS
Selchow & Righter 1959
Kids who were too young to read could still play this game.
$25 - $35

GINGERBREAD MAN
Selchow & Righter 1961
Cool game had four small puzzles of the gingerbread house that players had to be the first to finish.
$30 - $40

SIMPLE SIMON BALLOON GAME
Hasbro 1966
"With balloons."
$10 - $15

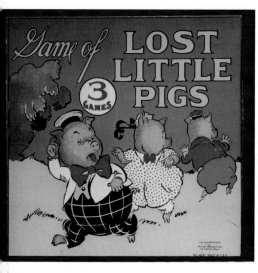

LOST LITTLE PIGS
Milton Bradley 1936
Three different simple games could be played on the box bottom board.
$30 - $40

FAIRY TALE GAME
Selchow & Righter 1962
Journey through a fairy tale kingdom. I don't like the way that wolf is looking at Little Red Riding Hood.
$10 - $15

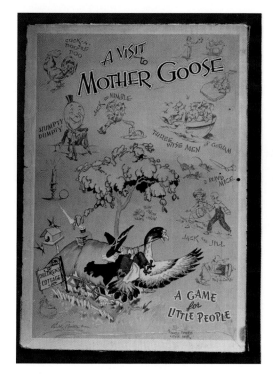

A VISIT TO MOTHER GOOSE
Parker Brothers 1947
Huge oversized game with beautiful artwork and chalk playing pieces of little boys and girls. I think it is one of the finest of the post-war era.
$75 - $95

HEX
Parker Brothers 1950
Build with "hex" shapes from one side of the board to the other. Neat Elf graphics.
$20 - $25

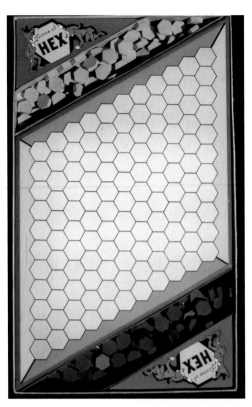

Inside of HEX.

AMAZE
Schuco Games 1976
Players plot mazes for their opponents.
Courtesy of Jeff Lowe's ExtravaGAMEza
$15 - $25

PEGITY
Parker Brothers 1930s
Another popular entrapment strategy game.
"Shall we play another?"
$20 - $25

WALKING BEANS
Unknown 1950s?
Weighted "beans" (like TUMBLEBUG) are coerced down the board to points.
$5

DAI JOBI
Parker Brothers 1956
"The Great Balinese Game." Basically, you throw colored sticks in the air and the way they come down determines play. Rare, obscure game.
$40 - $50

LANDMARKS
Selchow & Righter 196
Trivia game.
$15 - $20

COCKY COMPASS
Christian Toy Co. 1955
Interesting game of Palm Springs that has rules for play inside and outside. Includes a neat compass.
$25 - $35

PLAY USA
Harett-Gilmar 1950s
Neat trivia game where five
different knobs have to be aligned
correctly to get some answers.
$25 - $35

LET'S TAKE A TRIP
Milton Bradley 1963
Collector's seem to remember this game, as it's gets a lot of
requests. Players move their autos by spinning the dial.
Courtesy of Jeff Lowe's ExtravaGAMEza
$15 - $25

TRAVEL AMERICA
Jacmar 1950
Cheesy "electric" trivia game. Very small.
$15 - $20

GLOBE-TROTTERS
Selchow & Righter 1950
Directions are in comic strip form. Deadly words in
instructions: "you're sure to learn a lot."
$30 - $40

LLSTATE TRAVEL
lchow & Righter 1964
de exclusively for Sears, this neat car travel game
me with wooden cars and a built-in compass.
0 - $50

BILLBOARD
Harett-Gilmar 1956
"The Brand Name Advertising Game." Super cool game
involves buying advertising and renting billboard space.
Includes little wooden billboards of popular items.
$75 - $100

Inside of BILLBOARD.

Game Hunting?

At last all guess work has been eliminated in the selection of
the right game for the right age. The games in this folder have
been selected and classified for their appeal to various age
groups running the gamut from the toddling youngsters to the
doddering elder. Select any one of the several delightful Milton Bradley games from the proper age group and you will be
sure to select the right game for the right age. Milton Bradley
makes game hunting happy hunting for the entire family.

USE THIS
MILTON BRADLEY "GAME GUIDE"

PRICES IN THIS CIRCULAR MAY BE SLIGHTLY HIGHER IN THE WEST AND SOUTH.

FREEWAY
Plastic Art Toy Co. 1958
"Battery Operated 3-Dimensional Highway Game."
Courtesy of Jeff Lowe's ExtravaGAMEza
$50 - $60

HIGHWAY TRAFFIC
John Allison Jr. 1957
"Develops safe, thoughtful drivers."
Courtesy of Jeff Lowe's ExtravaGAMEza
$40 - $50

ZIPPITY SPEEDWAY
Kenner 1968
Battery operated game provided cushion of air for
Styrofoam cars to ride on, "Like the cars of tomorrow."
$50 - $60

TOWN AND COUNTRY TRAFFIC
Ranger Steel 1950s
Neat game came with metal autos and
metal traffic light "spinner."
$75 - $100

TRAFFIC
All-Fair 1930s
$45 - $55

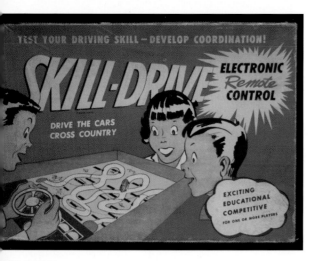

KILL-DRIVE
dney Tarrson Corp 1950s
Electronic Remote Control." I think not.
0 - $25

Strangers in the night.

RIVER TRAINING GAMES
ecor Note Co. 1959
o games, LET'S DRIVE and OLD SCRATCH. Cool, small
stic cars. In Old Scratch, the Devil tells you to do things like
ll asleep at the wheel," and "Pass on blind curves."
0 - $40

BREAKER 19
Milton Bradley 1976
"The CB Trucker's Game."
$10 - $15

UTOFUN
1F 1967
ge game, with battery operated scale cars. Same game as GET-
WAY CHASE GAME (see first book), which came out a year later.
5 - $100

KEEP ON TRUCKIN', AMERICA
Sandstorm Ent. 1976
Promotional game.
$10 - $15

DETOUR
American Greetings 1972
Rare game of world travel.
From the collection of Bob Claster
$40 - $50

BUILDING BOOM!
Kohner 1950
Moves were determined by putting a marble in the large
plastic "building" and seeing what came out.
Courtesy of Jeff Lowe's ExtravaGAMEza
$30 - $40

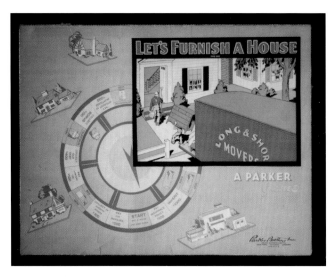

LET'S FURNISH A HOUSE
Parker Brothers 1947
Players spun to see which item they would get for the house. Sometimes they would have to pay repairs or insurance, sometimes they
would inherit money or collect an old debt. Large, scarce game.
$40 - $50

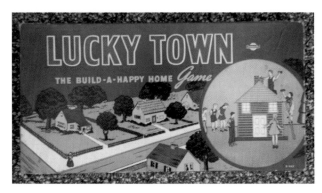

LUCKY TOWN
Somerville 1940s
Canadian. "The build-a-happy home game."
Courtesy of Jeff Lowe's ExtravaGAMEza
$40 - $60

BLACK COMMUNITY
M, Inc. 1967
"New exciting fun."... "What will you do when you get in a situation?"
$10 - $15

RATRACE
AMT 1968
"Madcap game of social climbing." Scarce game from a plastic
model company.
$20 - $30

INTERSECTION
Aladdin 1974
Game of Action and Reaction.
*Courtesy of Jeff Lowe's
ExtravaGAMEza*
$25 - $30

CROSS PURPOSES
Aladdin 1976
"The game of cross
and double-cross."
Scarce.
Courtesy of Jeff Lowe's
ExtravaGAMEza
$20 - $30

UP & ADD 'EM!
Aladdin 1976
"The sneaky game of conquest." From same series as CROSS
PURPOSES. Uncommon.
Courtesy of Jeff Lowe's ExtravaGAMEza
$20 - $30

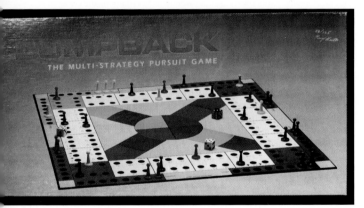

BUMPBACK
Butler Ind. 1983
The first 125 copies were signed and numbered.
$10 - $12

DOUBLETRACK
Milton Bradley 1981
Anyone could win in this mixed up
offering from Milton Bradley.
$10 - $15

LEVERAGE
Milton Bradley 1982
The object is to tilt the game board
down on your opponents side.
$10

SPECTRUM
Intellect Games 1975
"Colors clash for territorial gain."
The "Brief Encounter Games"
included WORDCROSS, QUITS,
CYPHER, and EGGHEAD.
Courtesy of Jeff Lowe's
ExtravaGAMEza
$10 - $12

QUITS
Intellect Games 1975
Game of positional cunning.
Courtesy of Jeff Lowe's ExtravaGAMEza
$10 - $12

CAMMY
Classic Games 1975
Historical game of the pre-Civil
War South.
Courtesy of Jeff Lowe's
ExtravaGAMEza
$15 - $20

REDSKIN FINGER PAINT
AGES 3 TO ADULT PRICE $2.00, OTHERS $1, $3
Here's fun for the entire family with America's largest selling finger paint. Available in 2 oz. or 4 oz. jars with either 6 of 6 colors—red, yellow, green, blue, brown and black. Finger paint paper, wooden spatulas and instructions included.

CANDY LAND
AGES 4 TO 8 PRICE $2.00, OTHER $1.00
Loads of fun and excitement as players advance along a Candy Land path through the Peppermint Stick Forest, Gum Drop Mountain and others. Nothing to read. This is an ideal first game for youngsters because of its interest. For 2, 3 or 4 players.

UNCLE WIGGILY
GES 4 TO 8 PRICE $2.00, OTHER $1.00
enerations of children have enjoyed the rills of helping dear old Uncle Wiggily nst the fox's den, through the cabbage tch and the snares of the forest in race to get their ailing friend to the ctor's office first. For 2, 3 or 4 players.

ZOO FUN
AGES 4 TO 9 PRICE $1.00
This fun at the zoo game teaches children to recognize the letters of the alphabet, to match sizes and shapes of objects, and how to spell and associate the letters with the animals. Contains beautiful die-cut illustrations of many zoo animals.

HIGGLY PIGGLY
Cadaco-Ellis 1956
Over 40 small plastic pieces! Kind of like Bingo. Super cool.
$40 - $50

TOP-OGRAPHY
Cadaco-Ellis 1947
Frightening geography game.
$25 - $30

Inside of HIGGLY PIGGLY.

OLD MOTHER HUBBARD
Cadaco-Ellis 1955
Companion game to LITTLE BOY BLUE (see first book).
$25 - $30

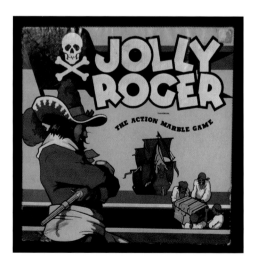

JOLLY ROGER
Cadaco-Ellis 1943
Marbles were dropped down a center chute and scored points. Another game of this style was DOWN THE HATCH.
$30 - $35

PINK ELEPHANT
Cadaco-Ellis 1941
Top game, early from
this company.
$20 - $25

RINGMASTER
Cadaco-Ellis 1947
Cool game with tons of cardboard circus animals. Scarce.
$40 - $50

OWN THE HATCH!
adaco-Ellis 1943
me game as JOLLY
OGER.
0 - $50

Inside of RING-
MASTER.

RANSPORT PILOT
adaco-Ellis 1938
0 - $75

SHARPSHOOTER
Cadaco-Ellis 1951
Original version.
$50- $60

SHARPSHOOTER
Cadaco 1962
$30 - $40

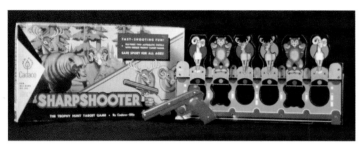

SHARPSHOOTER
Cadaco-Ellis 1962
Featured a pair of plastic, rubber band shooting guns. When you shot an animal, it would flip over revealing its point score. What I don't understand is how come on the box cover, all the animals are benign and smiling. Not just the ones on the wall, which might have been stuffed that way, but the ones in the forest, too. Yet on the target, they are all snarling with nasty expressions. Is it easier to kill an angry animal than a happy one?

HOOKEY
Cadaco-Ellis 1946
Catch those fish and put them in the cardboard frying pan.
$30 - $40

RED HERRING
Cadaco-Ellis 1944
Fish tile game with a "red herring" joker tile. I love all the Cadaco-Ellis games, but I think this is my favorite cover.
$30 - $45

TOP COP
Cadaco-Ellis 1961
Collect the bad guy tokens and become "Top Cop."
$35 - $45

Inside of TOP COP

LUCKY LOOPY
Cadaco-Ellis 1962
Large bean bag toss game
in which hitting a panel
reverses the scene for
often hilarious results.
*Courtesy of Jeff Lowe's
ExtravaGAMEza*
$40 - $50

GIANT STEPS
Milton Bradley 1957
Follow the leader.
$10 - $15

DOBBIN DERBY
Cadaco-Ellis 1950
Horse-race game with large cardboard horses.
$0 - $40

PONGO
Cadaco-Ellis 1953
Courtesy of Jeff Lowe's ExtravaGAMEza
$5 - $40

WATERWORKS
Parker Brothers 1976
Card game with tiny metal wrenches.
$10 - $15

GIANT STEP
Pressman 1960s
Try to jump from step to step
without being tagged.
*Courtesy of Jeff Lowe's
ExtravaGAMEza*
$15 - $20

TAG
Milton Bradley 1958
Believe it or not, a board game about "tag."
$0 - $15

POLLYANNA DIXIE
Parker Brothers 1954
Plays like PARCHEESI. Many different versions (see first book).
$20 - $25

MOVIE STUDIO MOGUL
International Marketing Consultants 1981
Run the studios.
$30 - $40

POLLYANNA
Parker Brothers 1951
Used to be called "The Glad Game."
$25 - $30

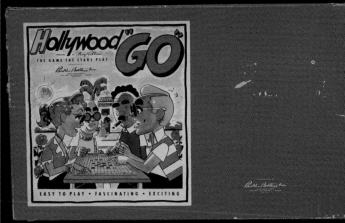

HOLLYWOOD GO
Parker Brothers 1954
"The game the stars play." GO game.
$30 - $40

HOLLYWOOD AWARDS
Milton Bradley 1976
"Glamorous game of stars, fame and fortune."
$25 - $30

SOCIETY SCANDA
E.S. Lowe 1978
Upper crust shenanig.
$20

MOVIE MOGULS
Research Games 1973
Scarce game.
*Courtesy of Jeff Lowe's
ExtravaGAMEza*
$50 - $60

Left:
MOVIE GAME
The Movie Game, Ltd. 1981
Trivia game.
$15 - $20

CHONCA
Hasbro 1950s
$30 - $40

JNE-IN TV BINGO
lchow & Righter 1970
ayers matched their bingo cards to
ages they saw on TV.
0 - $15

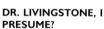

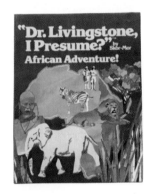

**DR. LIVINGSTONE, I
PRESUME?**
Skor-Mor 1970s
*Courtesy of Jeff Lowe's
ExtravaGAMEza*
$20 - $25

AFRICAN ANIMAL HUNT
Parker Brothers 1960
$50 - $60

AFRICAN ANIMAL HUNT
Parker Brothers 1960
Super cool game includes tons of colored plastic animals, although I don't see why
we have so many varieties of Goats, Sheep, and Horses if we're hunting in Africa.
Couldn't they afford the scarier animals? Beautiful cover for obscure game.

IAH-SHAH
rey Games 1930s
ategy game.
0 - $40

CRAZY FARM
Milton Bradley 1970
Regular track game. I wouldn't be holding hands with a lion if I was going somewhere called "Crazy Farm."
$7 - $10

FUN ON THE FARM
Milton Bradley 1950s
$15 - $20

FARM MANAGEMENT
Big Top 1962
Farm teaching tool.
$20

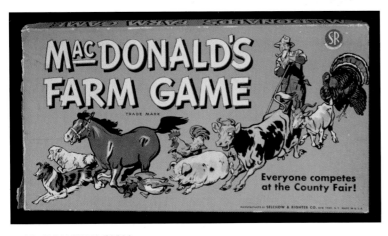

MacDONALD'S FARM
Selchow & Righter 1950s
All the animals compete at the county fair.
$20 - $22

Right:
BALDICER
John Knox Press 1970
Simulation game on world hunger.
Courtesy of Jeff Lowe's ExtravaGAMEza
$15 - $20

OVER THE GARDEN WALL
Parker Brothers 1940s
Similar TO BUNNY RABBIT. No relation to a Milton Bradley game of same name.
$25 - $30

HEE HAW
Cadaco 1970
Simple child's game. *Not* based on a TV show.
$10 - $15

R
chow & Righter 1977
oyal Game of Sumer." Replica of ancient Sumerian game.
0 - $15

AIR MAIL PILOT
Advance Games 1940s
Uncommon game came complete with all kinds of
air mail and air mail labels. Even stamps!
$55 - $75

SPHINX
Unknown 1970s
Courtesy of Jeff Lowe's ExtravaGAMEza
$20 - $25

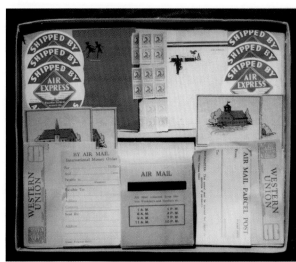

Inside of AIR MAIL PILOT.

NGAME
e Ungame Co. 1972
mmon game.
- $7

SHOULDER TO SHOULDER
Intellect Games 1975
Unique tactical game.
Courtesy of Jeff Lowe's ExtravaGAMEza
$15 - $20

FLYING THE BEAM
Parker Brothers 1941
Very Rare. Separate board and box
edition (see first book). Small
airplanes are composition instead
of metal, because of war-time
rationing.
From the collection of Bob Claster
$75 - $100

113

Inside of FLYING THE BEAM.

OVER THE RAINBOW SEE-SAW GAME
Milton Bradley 1949
Similar to BABAR AND HIS FRIENDS SEE-SAW
GAME.
Courtesy of Jeff Lowe's ExtravaGAMEza
$25 - $35

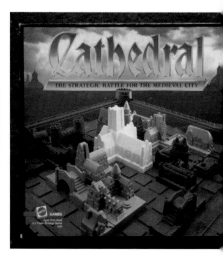

CATHEDRAL
Mattel 1986
$10 - $12

EAT AT RALPH'S
Milton Bradley 1992
Disgusting motorized game in which players try to feed as
much food as they can into a giant plastic mouth until it vomits
on a unlucky player. Putrid games like this sometimes become
collectible because most people shun them, and they end up on
the bargain tables.
$10

ARMAGEDDON
Everon International 1977
End of the world. Scarce.
Courtesy of Jeff Lowe's ExtravaGAMEza
$35 - $40

MAGIC THE GATHERING
Wizards of the Coast 1995
Starter pack that began the card playing craze
$20

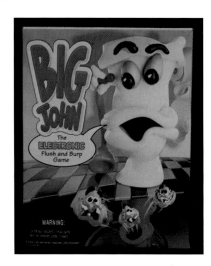

BIG JOHN
Parker Brothers 1994
Another revolting electronic game in which players try to stuff
things down a toilet, until it backs up and spews out filth. All kinds
of euphemisms are used to describe feces without actually naming
it. Again, so shunned that it may become collectible.
$10

VOYAGE TO CIPANGU
Cipangu Games Go. 1979
Beautiful board graphics, small 3-D sailing ships similar to BROADSIDES
AND BOARDING PARTIES. Scarce.
Courtesy of Jeff Lowe's ExtravaGAMEza
$50 - $75

CONQUEST OF THE RING
Hobbit Toys and Games Inc. 1970
Middle Earth adventure.
$25 - $35

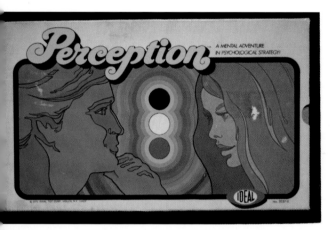

PERCEPTION
Ideal 1971
"Mental adventure." Unusual game for Ideal. Game is inside slipcover.
$20 - $25

IMPOSSIBLE GAME
Createk 1968
Bizarre strategy game.
$25 - $35

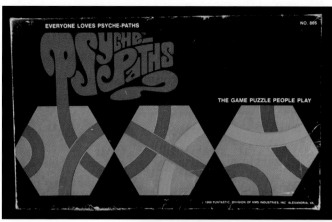

PSYCHE-PATHS
Funtastic 1969
Puzzle game.
$15 $20

PSYCHOBOARD
Happy Hour 1957
OUIJA-type game. For some reason, U.S. Steel Supply presented this game.
$25 - $30

SCAM
Brown Bag Enterprises 1971
Obscure, poorly made drug game.
From the collection of Bob Claster
$20 - $25

SCAM
Christenson Bros. 1978
Another cheesy drug game that, incredibly, is
unrelated to the earlier version of the same name.
From the collection of Bob Claster
$15 - $20

BEAT THE BUZZ
Kenner 1958
"It's fun to beat the buzz." If the metal
wand touches the metal track, it buzzes.
$15 - $20

**DEALER McDOPE DEAL-
ING GAME**
Last Gasp 1975
Rare game based on an under-
ground comic-book character
(from the Fabulous Freak
Brothers).
*Courtesy of Jeff Lowe's
ExtravaGAMEza*
$50 - $75

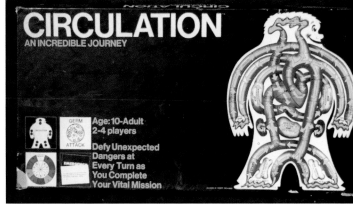

CIRCULATION
Teaching Concepts 1974
Disgusting game takes you on an "incredible journey" through the human
body. One of the few games with "Gaseous" and "Renal" waste cards.
From the collection of Bob Claster
$25 - $35

CHUG-A-LUG
Marina Enterprises 1969
Yep, it's a "hilarious drinking
game," with Alka-Seltzer "for
the morning after."
$20 - $25

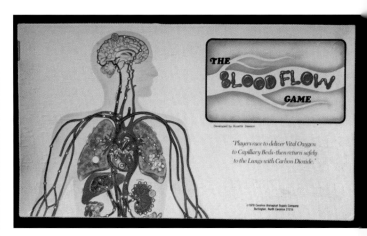

REFLEX
Lakeside 1966
"How quick can you think?
How fast can you act?"
$20

BLOOD FLOW
Carolina Biological Supply Co. 1978
Almost as disgusting as CIRCULATION, with cards that conserve the oxygen suppl
to the blood (Sleeping) or use it at an alarming rate (Your teacher wants to see you
$20 - $25

TRUNK FOR TRIVIA
Unknown 1980s
Trunk to carry your TRIVIAL
PURSUIT game in.
$10

**MYSTIQUE FORTELL
CARDS**
Mattel 1969
Fortune telling game, with
vinyl case and real groovy
graphics.
$20 - $25

OUIJA
William Fuld 1950s
The original "Talking Board."
$25 - $35

DIAL
Gardner Games 1950s
Rare game in which players gather up numbers to dial the telephone.
$30 - $40

MAGIC ROBOT QUIZ
Merit 1960s
English game, with same technology as ASK
THE VEDA. But this has a cool robot.
$35 - $45

FRONT PAGE
Gameophiles Unltd. 1974
Compose the front page of the "Mainstreet Herald."
Courtesy of Jeff Lowe's ExtravaGAMEza
$40 - $50

ZAP!
Skor-Mor 1970s
Courtesy of Jeff Lowe's ExtravaGAMEza
$15 - $20

Left:
POLICE STATE
Gameophiles Unltd. 1974
"Game of strategy and survival."
Courtesy of Jeff Lowe's ExtravaGAMEza
$40 - $50

OLDIES BUT GOODIES
Original Sound Records 1984
Music trivia game played on enclosed audio tapes. Might have been LP version too.
$25 - $35

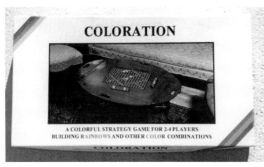

COLORATION
Gameophiles Unltd. 1973
Build rainbows.
Courtesy of Jeff Lowe's ExtravaGAMEza
$10 - $12

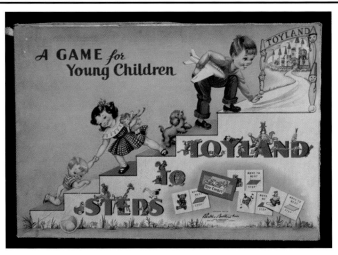

STEPS TO TOYLAND
Parker Brothers 1954
$40 - $55

FLIP & FLOP
Gameophiles Unltd. 1974
Courtesy of Jeff Lowe's ExtravaGAMEza
$12 - $15

SECRET TELEGRAM
Skor-Mor 1970s
Crack the code.
Courtesy of Jeff Lowe's ExtravaGAMEza
$20 - $25

STEPS TO TOYLAND
Parker Brothers 1954
This unusually large game had children rewarded with toys as they
moved up the steps toward Toyland. The board was beautifully illustrated, and the playing pieces were small kiddies made out of chalk.

KARATE
Selchow & Righter 1964
Card game in which players "Karate" each other, unless they
can save themselves with a "beetle" card. Scarce.
$25 - $35

TOY PARADE
Jaymar 1950s
If there was anything less in this box it would be empty.
$10 - $15

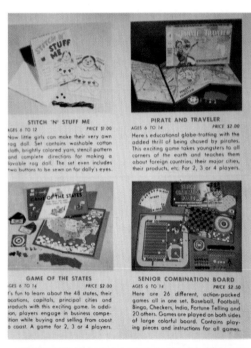

STITCH 'N' STUFF ME
AGES 6 TO 12   PRICE $1.00
Now little girls can make their very own
rag doll. Set contains washable cotton
cloth, brightly colored yarn, stencil pattern
and complete directions for making a
lovable rag doll. The set even includes
two buttons to be sewn on for dolly's eyes.

PIRATE AND TRAVELER
AGES 6 TO 14   PRICE $2.00
Here's educational globe-trotting with the
added thrill of being chased by pirates.
This exciting game takes youngsters to all
corners of the earth and teaches them
about foreign countries, their major cities,
their products, etc. For 2, 3 or 4 players.

GAME OF THE STATES
AGES 6 TO 14   PRICE $2.00
It's fun to learn about the 48 states, their
locations, capitals, principal cities and
products with this exciting game. In addition, players engage in business competition while buying and selling from coast
to coast. A game for 2, 3 or 4 players.

SENIOR COMBINATION BOARD
AGES 6 TO 14   PRICE $2.50
Here are 26 different, action-packed
games all in one set. Baseball, Football,
Bingo, Checkers, India, Fortune Telling and
20 others. Games are played on both sides
of large colorful board. Contains playing pieces and instructions for all games.

TOY STORE
Built-Rite 1950s
Courtesy of Jeff Lowe's ExtravaGAMEza
$20 - $25

GREAT AMERICAN FLAG GAME
Parker Brothers 1940
$55 - $75

GREAT AMERICAN FLAG GAME
Parker Brothers 1940
Super patriotic game which takes you through history and events involving the American flag. This version had one large forty-eight star cloth flag, while the later edition had six smaller (paper) flags. Unusual, scarce game.

GREAT AMERICAN FLAG GAME
Parker Brothers 1943
This edition came with six tiny paper flags.
$40 - $50

WORLD FLAG GAME
Parker Brothers 1961
Large, elaborate game about the flags of the United Nations.
$40 - $50

MEET THE PRESIDENTS
Selchow & Righter 1965
Quiz game with metal coin tokens. Later version (see first book).
$25 - $30

PRESIDENTIAL CONVENTION
Games Research 1960
Obscure political game.
From the collection of Bob Claster
$40 - $50

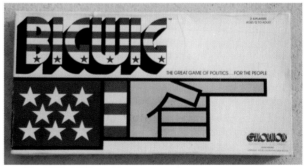

BIG WIG
Explorations, Inc. 1973
Courtesy of Jeff Lowe's ExtravaGAMEza
$25 - $35

BOONDOGGLE
Selchow & Righter 1952
Rare political game with very unusual box and board.
From the collection of Bob Claster
$50 - $65

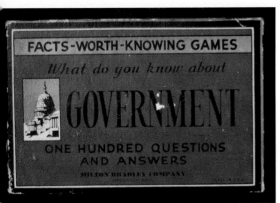

GOVERNMENT
Milton Bradley 1939
Boring trivia game.
From the collection of Bob Claster
$20 - $30

Right:
ELECTROMATIC DIAL QUIZ
Transogram 1961
What does "electromatic" mean? Uses
questions from "The Book of Knowledge" series of encyclopedia.
$25 - $35

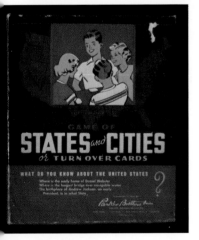

STATES AND CITIES
Parker Brothers 1957
"Or Turn Over Cards." Another
boring trivia game, this one about
states rather than the government.
$10 - $15

MR. BRAIN
Jacmar 1959
"The electronic answer man." Deluxe, double-sized version. When answers
were inserted into his mouth, colored lights in his eyes would light up. Neat.
$40 - $50

TRICK & TRAP
Everon International 1977
Rare Washington political power game.
Courtesy of Jeff Lowe's ExtravaGAMEza
$40 - $50

Inside of MR. BRAIN.

THINK-A-TRON
Hasbro 1961
$75 - $100

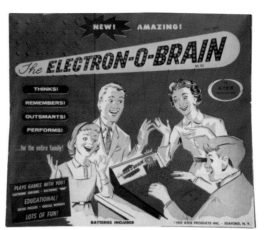

Left:
ELECTRON-O-BRAIN
Atex Products 1957
Batteries were included with this game!
Courtesy of Jeff Lowe's ExtravaGAMEza
$25 - $40

Below:
QWIK QWIZ
Transogram 1958
If you can see which slot the ball is falling into, and you match the answer quickly and correctly, you score points.
$25 - $35

THINK-A-TRON
Hasbro 1961
"The machine that thinks like a man." Super cool electronic question and answer plastic computer, long before anything like this was on the market. You stuck in little IBM punch cards and, after a period of flashing lights and noise, the machine displays the answer in lights. All questions were compiled from The Book of Knowledge Encyclopedia. You can just see James T. Kirk talking it into destroying itself.

Right:
QUIZ WIZ
Coleco 1978
True "electronic" computer quiz game.
$20 - $25

Below:
GUESS AGAIN
Milton Bradley 1967
An electric Question and Answer quiz game.
Courtesy of Rick Polizzi
$15 - $25

QUIZZIAC
Golden Capitol 1960
"The Question and Answer Machine with the Magnetic Brain." Small version of ASK THE VEDA. Questions by Golden.
$25 - $35

THE GLAMOROUS GAME OF STARS FAME AND FORTUNE

Right:
FIREBALL XL5
Milton Bradley 1964
$125 - $150

FIREBALL XL5
Milton Bradley 1964
Another entry from British puppeteer Gerry Anderson, this TV show followed the exploits of Steve Zodiac and his crew as they zoomed around space in their spaceship Fireball XL5. This TV show appeared after the series *SUPERCAR*, but before *STINGRAY* and *THUNDERBIRDS*—all popular "Super Marionation" adventures. In this game, Steve Zodiac, Venus, Professor, and Zero control two robot pieces each. The object is for each player to get his robots through the treacherous training course and into the "Robot Garage." Great graphics.

People want to be entertained, and industries have tried to pro-
de amusements through the media of print, radio, movies and
evision. Board games have frequently tried to translate that mass
edia experience in a way that enables people to relive their fa-
rite moments from entertainment in the comfort of their homes.
hile some games have been successful in this endeavor, like
rett-Gilmar's TREASURE ISLAND, with its elaborate magnetic
vices, metal sailing ship and cool compasses, more often they
ve failed—the game being nothing more than a marketing de-
e to exploit a current fad. Parker Brother's lame BONANZA
ard game falls into this category. The box cover shows the
rtwright family seated around a table playing cards with an obvi-
sly pasted on picture of the game in the center. The game was
thing more than plain old Michigan Rummy, with no reference
the show other than the phony cover.

Here then, good and bad, are the games inspired by films, books,
evision, toys, cartoons, comic books, comic strip characters,
ents, personalities, video games and even candy.

Prepare to be entertained!

STINGRAY
Transogram 1966
$250 - $300

LAND OF THE GIANTS
Ideal 1968
Based on the ABC TV show. Players had to collect items to repair their spaceship and avoid being captured by "Giants."
$125 - $150

STINGRAY
Transogram 1966
Based on the Saturday morning TV series using the "Super Marionation" process pioneered by Britian's Gerry Anderson. Basically a bunch of cool looking puppets, led by cool lead puppet Troy Tempest. Using the futuristic submarine STINGRAY, they would fight the evil Aquaphibians. In the game, the object was to reach the underwater city. A transparent maze device that attached to the board kept players shifting back and forth. One of the best looking game covers of the 1960s.

SEA HUNT
Lowell 1961
Based on the TV series starring Lloyd Bridges. Underwater treasure hunt.
$75 - $100

TIME TUNNEL
Ideal 1966
Based on the ABC TV series starring James Darren.
Players had to go back in time in this cool game.
$150 - $175

Inside of SEA HUNT.

QUANAUTS
ansogram 1961
sed on the CBS TV series starring Keith Larson. Underwater treasure hunt.
0 - $85

MISSION IMPOSSIBLE
Ideal 1966
Based on the CBS TV series starring Peter Graves as Jim Phelps. The impossible mission is finding this game, as it is quite uncommon.
$125 - $150

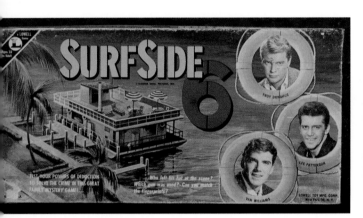

URFSIDE 6
well 1962
sed on the TV show starring Troy Donahue. Came with a magnify-
glass to help you match fingerprints and solve crimes.
5 - $75

THE FUGITIVE
Ideal 1964
Based on the ABC TV series starring David Janssen looking for the One-Armed Man. There is a rarer version of this game that has a small black and white photo of Janssen on the cover.
$150 - $175. Rarer version with Janssen photo: $225 - $250

IRONSIDE
Ideal 1967
Based on the NBC TV series starring Raymond Burr. Playing pieces are from Ideal's JAMES BOND MESSAGE FROM "M" GAME (see first book). It appears that everyone on the cover is using Ironside as a shield. Rare game.
$125 - $150

ONEY WEST
al 1965
he Girl Private-Eye." Based on the ABC TV series starring
ne Francis. Sort of a female *MAN FROM UNCLE*.
00 - $150

GREEN HORNET
Milton Bradley 1966
"Quick Switch Game." Super neat game based on the ABC TV series starring Van Williams, and Bruce Lee as Kato. Beautifully made game that has four built in "switches" that enable players to quickly move from one area to another. Hard to find game, with some great interior art.
$250 - $300

BURKE'S LAW
Transogram 1964
Based on the ABC TV show starring Gene Barry. Wealthy playboy solves murders.
$50 - $75

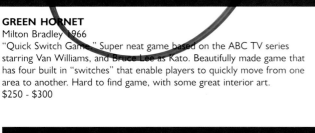

Inside of GREEN HORNET.

THE DETECTIVES
Transogram 1961
Based on the ABC TV series starring Robert Taylor. Identical game and artwork to Transogram's PHILIP MARLOWE GAME (see first book), except Robert Taylor is seen reaching for a fancy car phone rather than a gun. Transogram recycled more of its games than anyone else, in most cases barely even changing the cover art. They must have thought kids were either really bored or really stupid.
$35 - $55

Right:
HIGHWAY PATROL
Bell 1959
British game based on the popular TV series starring Broderick Crawford.
$75 - $100

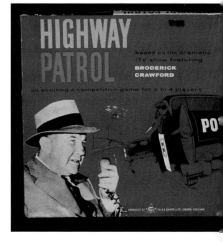

ARREST AND TRIAL
Transogram 1963
Based on the obscure ABC TV series starring Ben Gazzara and Chuck Connors. The same game as PERRY MASON and DRAGNET, which have identical covers (see first book).
$50 - $75

CHIPS
Milton Bradley 1978
Based on the TV series about the California Highway Patrol. This game is harder to find then the Ideal version put out at the same time (see first book).
$20 - $25

126

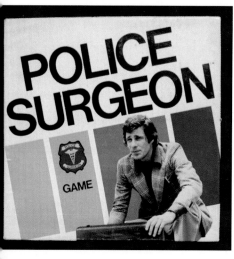

Right:
ADVENTURES OF SIR LANCELOT
Lisbeth-Whiting 1957
Based on the NBC TV series about Knights around the round table. Comes complete with Alligator Trap and Dragon Pit.
$75 - $100

POLICE SURGEON
American Publishing 1972
VERY obscure game based on the series starring Sam Groom (did it *ever* air?). This game was only available through mail order and is very rare for a variety of reasons.
$50 - $75

RAMAR OF THE JUNGLE
Dexter Wayne 1953
Cool game based on the TV show starring Jon Hall. Included a "Safari Scout" membership card.
$75 - $100

ADVENTURES OF LASSIE
Lisbeth-Whiting 1955
Hard to find game based on the CBS TV series. The game included four rubber "squeakers" which are almost always deteriorated. Beautiful box cover.
$55 - $75

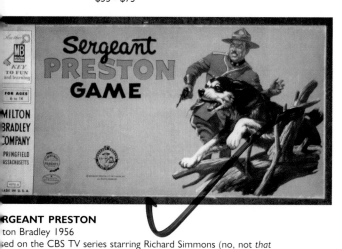

SERGEANT PRESTON
Milton Bradley 1956
Based on the CBS TV series starring Richard Simmons (no, not *that* Richard Simmons) and his dog King. Players advanced around the board trying to "always get their man." Common game.
$25 - $35

BIG TOWN
Lowell 1955
"News Reporting & Printing Game." Based on the TV series starring Mark Stevens. Players could actually print their own headlines on newspaper. Rare game.
Courtesy of Rick Polizzi
$75 - $100

GENTLE BEN ANIMAL HUNT
Mattel 1967
Based on the TV series about a Boy and his Bear.
This was one of a series of large "3-D" board games
by Mattel that included BARBIE WORLD OF FASH-
ION, DOCTOR DOLITTLE, and MAJOR MATT
MASON SPACE EXPLORATION GAME.
Courtesy of Rick Polizzi
$50 - $75

Right:
IT'S ABOUT TIME
Ideal 1965
Very rare game based
on the CBS TV series
about astronauts
trapped in the Stone
Age. Same game as
Ideal's KING ZOR (see
first book).
$200 - $250

GRIZZLY ADAMS
House of Games 1978
"Save the Animals Adventure Game." Based
on the TV show about a Mountain Man.
$15 - $20

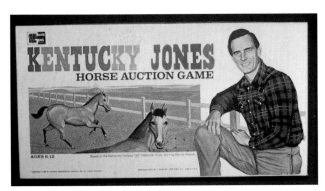

KENTUCKY JONES HORSE AUCTION GAME
Game Gems 1965
Based on the NBC TV series starring Dennis Weaver. This is
the short-lived show for which he left *GUNSMOKE*. One of the
very few games made by this company, all of them rare.
Courtesy of Rick Polizzi
$55 - $75

GIDGET
Standard Toykraft 1965
Based on the TV series starring Sally Fields as the "Girl-Midget."
Players had to match up tiles to form a complete person. GIDGET
FORTUNE TELLER GAME also exists (see first book).
$75 - $100

Below:
FAMILY AFFAIR
Whitman 1971
Based on the CBS TV
show starring Brian Keith.
Insubstantial game in
which players vie to be
the first to find "Mrs.
Beasley."
$40 - $50

ANGELA CARTWRIGHT BUTTONS 'N BOWS
Transogram 1960
Based on "America's little darling" appearing on CBS TV's *Danny Thomas Show*. She is probably better known as Penny from *LOST IN SPACE*. "Who will be first to pick and match Angela's 'Magic Buttons 'n Bows'?" Rare game.
From the collection of Michael Quinn
$75 - $100

LOVE BOAT
Ungame 1980s
"World Cruise Game." Based on the popular inane TV series. "Score points with the crew of the Love Boat."
$15 - $20

WELCOME BACK KOTTER CARD GAME
Milton Bradley 1976
Based on the "Up your nose with a rubber hose" TV series. There was also a game by Ideal (see first book).
$15 - $20

ROWAN & MARTIN'S OFFICIAL LAUGH-IN SQUEEZE YOUR BIPPY GAME
Hasbro 1968
Based on the popular TV show. Game had players performing stunts and "squeezing their bippys," a plastic toy bottle with squeaker, in the hopes of blowing a ball from one opponents color to another.
$40 - $50

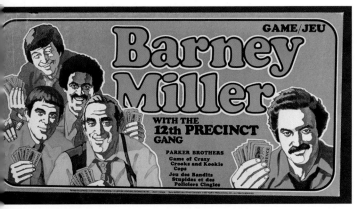

BARNEY MILLER
Parker Brothers 1977
Canadian version. Based on the TV series starring Hal Linden (see first book). I don't know French but it looks like "crazy" translates as "stupid."
Courtesy of R. Cautela
$25 - $35

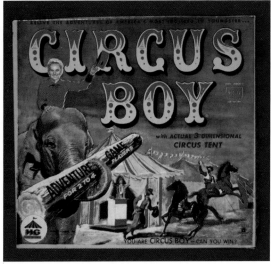

CIRCUS BOY
Harett-Gilmar 1956
Based on the NBC TV series starring Micky Dolenz (of THE MONKEES) about a boy in the circus.
$55 - $75

HUCK FINN
Transogram 1969
Based on the NBC TV show that mixed live action with animation. Scarce game.
$35 - $45

HARDY BOYS MYSTERY GAME
Parker Brothers 1978
"Secret of Thunder Mountain." Based on the ABC TV series starring Parker Stevenson and Shaun Cassidy, from the popular book series. There was an animated series too (see first book).
$15 - $25

BUGALOOS
Milton Bradley 1971
Based on the Sid & Marty Krofft TV series. Highly sought after by music collectors.
$35 - $45

MIGHTY MORPHIN POWER RANGERS
Milton Bradley 1993
Based on the horribly popular toys and TV program. Possible future collectible.
$10 - $15

WONDERBUG
Ideal 1977
Another Sid & Marty Krofft TV show about a Dune Buggy "Schlep" who turns into "Wonderbug." Players had to put together puzzle pieces of the bug.
$25 - $35

DONNY & MARIE OSMOND TV SHOW
Mattel 1976
Based on TV variety show starring the cheerful du
From the collection of Bob Claster
$30 - $40

THAT'S INCREDIBLE!
MPH 1970s
Small, obscure game based on the TV series.
$15 - $25

Left:
**SATURDAY NIGHT
LIVE TRIVIA GAME**
Tiger 1993
Trivial Pursuit-style
based on the popular
TV series.
$25 - $30

POLE POSITION
Parker Brothers 1983
Based on the arcade racing game.
From the collection of Bob Claster
$10 - $15

FROGGER
Milton Bradley 1981
Based on the disgusting video arcade
game about a frog trying to cross traffic.
$15 - $25

DONDI PRAIRIE RACE
Hasbro 1960
Based on the comic strip character. Three games were made, including
DONDI POTATO RACE, and DONDI FINDERS KEEPERS.
Courtesy of Rick Polizzi
$30 - $40

Q*BERT
Parker Brothers 1983
Based on the arcade game.
$15 - $20

DONDI FINDERS KEEPERS
Hasbro 1960
Based on the comic strip character. Came with plastic rocks.
$40 - $50

POPEYE'S 3 GAME SET
Built-Rite 1956
Slight three-in-one game based on
the popular cartoon character.
$30 - $40

131

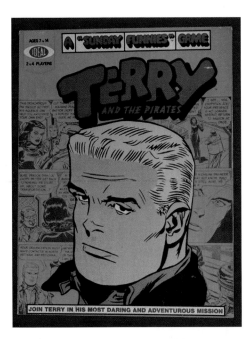

Left:
TERRY AND THE PIRATES
Ideal 1972
Based on the comic strip. One of Ideal's "Sunday Funnies" games, which included REX MORGAN M.D., BLONDIE, and MARY WORTH.
$30 - $15

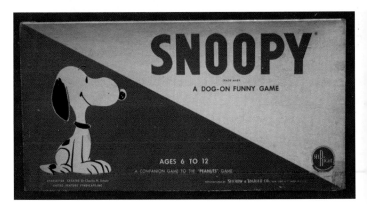

SNOOPY
Selchow & Righter 1960
"A Dog-On Funny Game." Based on the popular comic-strip character, companion game to PEANUTS (see first book).
$50 - $75

REX MORGAN M.D.
Ideal 1972
Based on the comic strip.
$30 - $40

LITTLE ORPHAN ANNIE PURSUIT GAME
Selchow & Righter 1978
Obscure track game based on the comic strip character.
$20 - $25

ELLA CINDERS
Milton Bradley 1944
Rare game based on th[e] comic strip characters
Courtesy of Jeff Lowe's ExtravaGAMEza
$75 - $125

DICK TRACY SUPER DETECTIVE MYSTERY CARD GAME
Whitman 1941
Card game based on the comic strip character.
$20 - $30

BLONDIE
Parker Brothers 1969
Based on the comic-strip characters (see first book).
$25 - $35

Left:
RANGER RICK AND THE GREAT FOREST FIRE
National Wildlife Federation
1960
Beautiful game based on Government public service character (similar to Smokey the Bear). Created by John A. Morris. Illustrated by Lorin Thompson.
$125 - $150

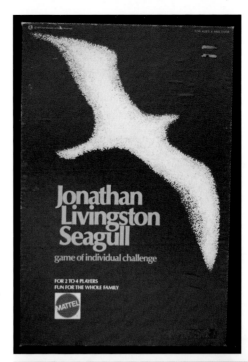

JONATHAN LIVINGSTON SEAGULL
Mattel 1973
$20 - $25

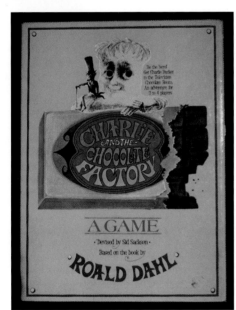

CHARLIE AND THE CHOCOLATE FACTORY
Knopf 1978
Based on the classic book by Roald Dahl. This neat game looks like a book, but folds out into a game board and pieces.
From the collection of Bob Baster
$75 - $100

JONATHAN LIVINGSTON SEAGULL
Mattel 1973
Beautiful game based on the incongruously best selling book. Plastic seagull pieces followed a circular path towards the center of the board, and enlightenment. The spinner was also a plastic seagull, and determined your moves.

AND THEN THERE WERE NONE
Ideal 1967
"An Agatha Christie Mystery Game." From the Famous Mystery Classic Series, which included THE CASE OF THE ELUSIVE ASSASSIN, MURDER ON THE ORIENT EXPRESS, and FU MANCHU'S HIDDEN HOARD (see first book). Playing pieces were from Ideal's JAMES BOND MESSAGE FROM "M" GAME.
$65 - $75

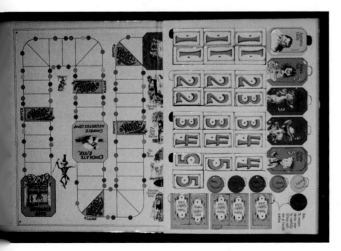

Inside of CHARLIE AND THE CHOCOLATE FACTORY.

ALICE IN WONDERLAND
Parker Brothers 1930s
Box bottom board game based on the novel which has
players trying to spell out Alice's name with letter tiles.
$50 - $75

ROBINSON CRUSOE
Lowell 1961
Based on the novel. Magnetic playing features, similar
to TREASURE ISLAND by Harett-Gilmar.
$75 - $100

TOM SWIFT
Parker Brothers 1966
$50 - $75

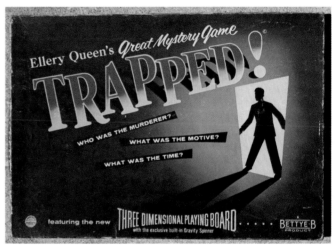

TRAPPED!
Bettye-B 1956
"Ellery Queen's Great Mystery Game." Based on the Ellery
Queen novels, three dimensional playing board. Scarce.
Courtesy of Rick Polizzi
$50 - $75

TOM SWIFT
Parker Brothers 1966
Based on the popular adventure books. Neat game came with plastic
"Polar-Ray Dynasphere," the space ship Tom flew around in. Players
went from Land, Sea, Air, and Space to pick up plans for the Polar-Ray
Dynasphere gun, at which point they could fire it at will.

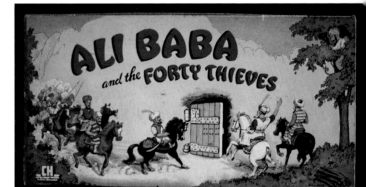

ALI BABA AND THE FORTY THIEVES
Craig Hopkins Co. 1945
Based on *The Arabian Nights*. The game has lots of neat little cardboard pieces.
$40 - $50

134

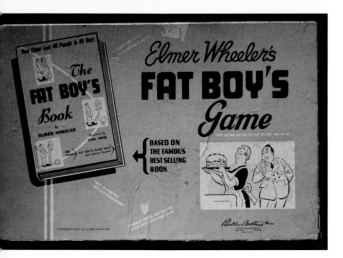

ELMER WHEELER'S FAT BOY'S GAME
Parker Brothers 1951
"Based on the best selling book." Game emphasizes proper diet. Pawns are "fat."
$35 - $45

BABAR AND HIS FRIENDS SEE-SAW GAME
Milton Bradley 1961
Based on the children's books. Similar to OVER THE RAINBOW SEE-SAW GAME. It's interesting to note that the loser is the one who's end of the see-saw is lowered into the alligator swamp.
$40 - $50

DANA GIRLS
Parker Brothers 1966
Based on the children's books. Only available in Canada. Rare.
$75 - $100

RUDOLPH THE RED-NOSED REINDEER
Parker Brothers 1940s
"Stick the Nose on..." Pin the tail on the donkey variant, based on the book by R.L. May.
$45 - $55

HARDY BOYS TREASURE GAME
Parker Brothers 1957
Based on the popular children's books. Same game as Disney version, with slightly different cover art.
$30 - $40

CHARLOTTE'S WEB
Hasbro 1976
Canadian. Based on the TV program of the book.
$40 - $45

CAPTAIN AMERICA
Milton Bradley 1966
Based on the Marvel comic book hero. Included a "free" comic book, which is almost never there.
$75 - $100 (with comic book)

SPIDER-MAN
Milton Bradley 1967
Based on the Marvel hero. Neat graphics of Thor, Sub-Mariner, Hulk, and Iron Man. The 1977 game with the Fantastic Four (see first book) is almost exactly the same; only the portraits in corners of the board are different.
$75 - $100

SUPERMAN SPEED GAME
Milton Bradley 1940
Very rare game is the first based on the DC Comics popular superhero.
$350 - $450

MIGHTY HEROES ON THE SCENE
Transogram 1966
Rare game based on the obscure animated TV series.
$125 - $150

SUPERMAN
Hasbro 1965
"Search for Superman's Deadliest Enemy." Rare game that pits Superman against Lex Luthor.
$75 - $100

MIGHTY COMICS SUPER HEROES GAME
Transogram 1966
The 1940s super heroes revived for a time in Archie Comics.
$100 - $150

SUPERMAN AND SUPERBOY GAM
Milton Bradley 1967
"2 Super Games in One."
$45 - $55

SUPERBOY
Hasbro 1965
Has Super Dog Krypto tagging along.
$75 - $90

SUPERMAN FLYING BINGO
Whitman 1966
Cheesy game in which players toss small "S" chips into a plastic tray and try to bingo with colors.
$25 - $35

THE FLASH
Hasbro 1967
"Justice League of America." Scarce series from Hasbro that included WONDER WOMAN and AQUAMAN. Very simple games.
Courtesy of Rick Polizzi
$200 - $250

[SH]AZAM
[Re]ed & Assoc. 1940s
["C]aptain Marvel's Own Game." Flat envelope game in which [pla]yers compete to make a Billy Batson or Captain Marvel figure.
[$]0 - $50

WONDER WOMAN
Hasbro 1967
Rare game.
$175 - $225

BATMAN CARD GAME
Ideal 1966
$40 - $50

SUPERMAN CARD GAME
Ideal 1966
$30 - $40

AQUAMAN
Hasbro 1967
Rarest of the series.
Courtesy of Rick Polizzi
$275 - $300

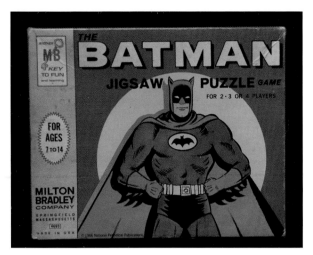

BATMAN JIGSAW
Milton Bradley 1966
$40 - $45

BATMAN JIGSAW PUZZLE GAME
Milton Bradley 1966
Based on the comic book character. Players stuck their hands into an opening in the box and selected puzzle pieces. First player to assemble a picture of Batman (from the Milton Bradley game cover art) was the winner.

INCREDIBLE HULK SMASH-UP ACTION GAME
Ideal 1979
Based on the Marvel comics character. Almost a toy, the set included a motorized Hulk who went on the rampage and destroyed property.
$30 - $40

Close up of "Motorized Hulk."

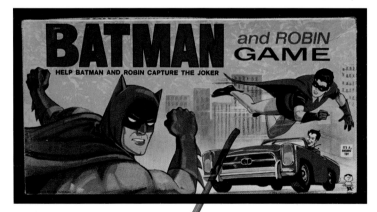

BATMAN AND ROBIN
Hasbro 1966
"Help Batman and Robin Capture the Joker." Robin appears to be flying on the cover.
$75 - $95

BILLY BLASTOFF SPACE GAME
Danlee 1969
Very small game based on the Eldon toy put out as competition for Mattel's Major Matt Mason.
$30 - $40

Left:
MAJOR MATT MASON SPACE EXPLORATION GAME
Mattel 1967
Cool game based on a toy. The game was part of Mattel's 3-D series, which included BARBIE WORLD OF FASHION, DOCTOR DOLITTLE, and GENTLE BEN.
Courtesy of Rick Polizzi
$75 - $100

BARBIE MISS LIVELY LIVIN'
Mattel 1970
"Share all the excitement of Barbie's swinging world and you could become Miss Lively Livin'." One of many games based on Mattel's popular doll (see first book). Winner got to wear the Lively Livin' crown!
$40 - $50

G.I. JOE NAVY FROGMAN!
Hasbro 1965
Based on the Hasbro toy. Others in the series included COMBAT INFANTRY, MARINE PARATROOPER, and RIK-O-SHAY GAME (see first book).
$50 - $65

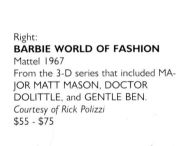

Inside of BARBIE MISS LIVELY LIVIN'.

CR-UNCH!
Mattel 1967
"With the Creeple Peeple." This cool game may never have been released.
Courtesy of Rick Polizzi
$75 - $100

Right:
BARBIE WORLD OF FASHION
Mattel 1967
From the 3-D series that included MAJOR MATT MASON, DOCTOR DOLITTLE, and GENTLE BEN.
Courtesy of Rick Polizzi
$55 - $75

FLATSY
Ideal 1970
Very scarce game based on the popular doll made by Ideal.
$75 - $95

TAFFY'S SHOPPING SPREE
Transogram 1964
Based on a created character. From the series that included
TAFFY'S PARTY GAME and TAFFY'S BAUBLES & BANGLES.
$20 - $25

TOOTY FROOTY
Hasbro 1960s
"The New Mr. Potato Head Game." Cool game based on the
Hasbro favorite. Plays like COOTIE, with spinner determining
which piece goes on what part of the body. Includes Pete The
Pepper, Cooky the Cucumber, and a Carrot creature.
$50 - $75

TAFFY'S PARTY GAME
Transogram 1964
$20 - $25

CHICLETS GUM VILLAGE
Hasbro 1969
Based on the popular candy. Winner gets one of six included boxes of
Chiclet's Gum. My dentist advises against eating 40 year old gum.
$25 - $35

TAFFY'S BAUBLES & BANGLES
Transogram 1964
$25 - $30

TOOTSIE ROLL TRAIN GAME
Hasbro 1969
Based on yummy candy. Another game where the
winner gets a treat, a Tootsie Roll candy in this case.
$30 - $40

[EL]SIE AND HER FAMILY
[Sel]chow & Righter 1941
[Th]e Junior Edition of a full size game based on the Borden cow.
[$?]0 - $55

Right:
**[C]AMPBELL KIDS
[SH]OPPING
[G]AME**
[Par]ker Brothers
[?]55
[Scar]ce game based
[on] the Soup twins.
[Wi]nner was in the
[sha]pe of a
[Ca]mpbell kid.
[$?]00 - $150

The Clairol Beauty Game

CLAIROL BEAUTY GAME
American Publishing 1969
Salon training game where operators tried to get the most customers. Scarce.
$25 - $30

Right:
**NATIONAL
ENQUIRER GAME**
Tyco 1990
Game based on the scandal sheet became popular for a short time after Princess Di's death (one person was asking $10,000). Same thing happened to Ideal's 1976 SINKING OF THE TITANIC GAME after the movie came out (see first book).
$15 - $20

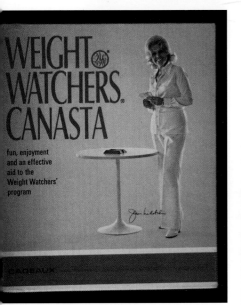

[W]EIGHT WATCHERS CANASTA
[Mil]ton Bradley/Cadeaux 1972
[Mil]ton Bradley's adult division produced this game
[ba]sed on the diet program that had players combine
[car]ds to produce weekly menus.
[$?]0 - $25

PAN AMERICAN WORLD JET FLIGHT GAME
Hasbro 1956
"Pilot a Jet Clipper to all six continents of the world." Neat plastic airplanes.
$30 - $40

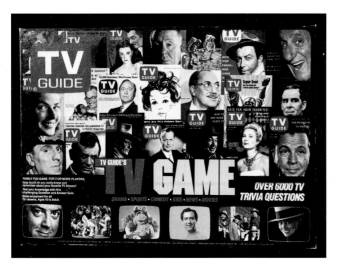

TV GUIDE'S TV GAME
Trivia, Inc. 1984
TV trivia game.
$10 - $15

XAVIERA'S HAPPY HOOKER GAME
Reiss 1976
"The Oldest Game in the World." Inspired by the famous Madam Xaviera Hollander.
From the collection of Bob Claster
$20 - $25

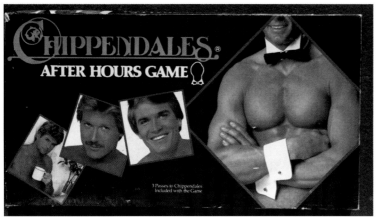

CHIPPENDALES AFTER HOURS GAME
Diplomat Games 1983
Based on the famous strip joint. Came with three free passes to the club.
$15 - $20

LITTLE BLACK SAMBO
Cadaco-Ellis 1951
Courtesy of Rick Polizzi
$150 - $200

LITTLE BLACK SAMBO
Cadaco Ellis 1951
Beautiful board game based on the colorful character. Although the implements are simple, the wonderful cover and board game design make this a constant favorite among collectors. Players try to make it past all the tigers and get home to pancake

BOZO THE CLOWN CIRCUS GAME
Transogram 1960
Based on the famous Larry Harmon clown
$30 - $40

OZO THE CLOWN IN CIRCUS LAND
Lowell 1965
Courtesy of Rick Polizzi
$45 - $55

LOWELL THOMAS' TRAVEL GAME
Parker Brothers 1937
You could get a hernia from lifting this enormous game based on the exploits of "World Traveler, Author, Radio Commentator" Lowell Thomas.
$75 - $100

EMMETT KELLY'S CIRCUS GAME
All-Fair 1953
Funny game based on the famous circus clown.
$30 - $40

Right:
EDDIE CANTOR'S NEW GAME TELL IT TO THE JUDGE
Parker Brothers 1932
"Club Game." This is the original version of this game (see first book).
$45 - $55

THE 3 STOOGES FUN HOUSE GAME
Lowell 1959
Very rare and very fun game based on the antics of the original three members.
$300 - $375

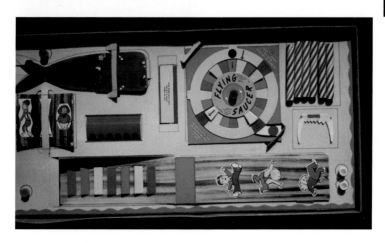

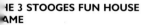
Inside of THE 3 STOOGES FUN HOUSE GAME.

Left:
TINY TIM THE GAME OF BEAUTI-FUL THINGS
Parker Brothers 1970
Game based on a bizarre TV personality.
$50 - $75

BORIS KARLOFF'S MONSTER GAME
Game Gems 1965
Very rare game based on "monster" actor Boris
Karloff. From a small line of board games.
$200 - $250

STEVE ALLEN'S QUBILA
Lord & Freber, Inc
1955
Teaches young
children to spell an
add.
$25 - $35

Left:
**FLIP-IT TWENT
ONE**
Aurora 1973
Flip Wilson lent his
name to the "Flip-
series that include
FLIP-IT JACKPOT
(see first book).
$30 - $40

UNDERSEA WORLD OF JACQUES COUSTEAU
Parker Brothers 1968
Based on the famous undersea explorer.
$30 - $40

BODY LANGUAGE
Milton Bradley 1975
"The Party Pantomime Word Game." Lucille Ball
appears on the cover. She's also on the cover of
Milton Bradley's CROSS UP (see first book).
$15 - $20

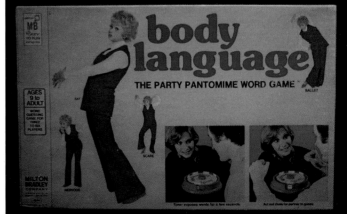

IVOT POOL
ton Bradley 1972
ries created to compete with Aurora's line of Skittle
oducts. There was also PIVOT GOLF (originally released as
bley's GOLFERINO). Lucille Ball appeared on the cover.
urtesy of Rick Polizzi
0 - $40

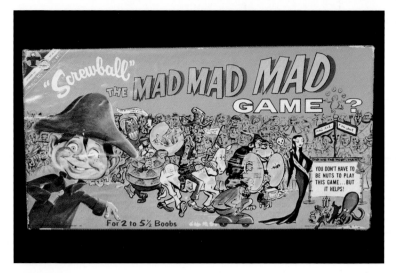

SCREWBALL
Transogram 1958
This is the original version of this game in which *Mad Magazine* sued
for copyright infringement (see first book for revised game).
$40 - $50

IGLE DINGLE'S WEATHER GAME
well 1954
0 - $125

WHIRLIGIG
Milton Bradley 1963
"Inspired by Art Linkletter on his
famous 'House Party' program."
$25 - $35

IGLE DINGLE'S WEATHER GAME
vell 1954
me was based on weather puppet Jingle Dingle (would *you* trust the
ather being given to you by a puppet? I guess forecasts are frequently
ccurate no matter who is delivering them). Players tried to rid their states
asty weather conditions. Included Jingle Dingle's weather station. Rare.

DUNGEONS & DRAGONS
Mattel 1980
From Mattel's Electronic series, a beautiful game
with miniature warrior figures and a scary dragon.
$20 - $30

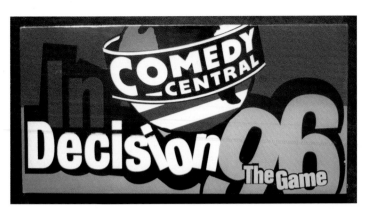

COMEDY CENTRAL INDECISION 96
Unknown 1996
Scarce promo game of 1996
Presidential race.
Courtesy of R. Cautela
$25 - $35

Right:

THE WATERGATE SCANDAL GAME
America Symbolic 1973
Scarce game of "cover-up and deception for the whole family."
$25 - $35

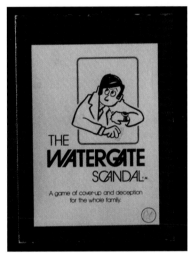

EXPLORING
Parker Brothers 1963
Based on the NBC "Educational" TV series.
$25 - $35

DISCOVERY
Lowell 1960s
Based on the ABC Educational TV series. There must have been other editions. This one is based on Geography.
$25 - $30

RIPLEY'S BELIEVE IT OR NOT!
Whitman 1979
Cool game with 44 "Believe It or Not!" fact cards.
$25 - $30

CRUSADE
Games for Industry
1967
Cancer research benefit game.
Courtesy of Jeff Lowe's ExtravaGAMEza
$30 - $40

HOME
Pressman 1950
"Official game of NBC TV HOME show." With Arlene Francis and Hugh Downs as hosts.
Courtesy of Jeff Lowe's ExtravaGAMEza
$40 - $65

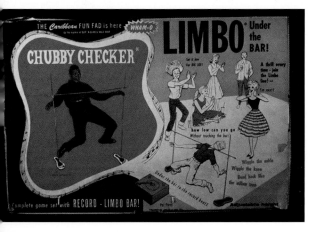

CHUBBY CHECKER LIMBO
Wham-O 1961
"The Caribbean Fun Fad is here." Chubby Checker lent his name and image to this game previously released by Wham-O. Came with "Limbo" record.
Courtesy of Rick Polizzi
$50 - $60

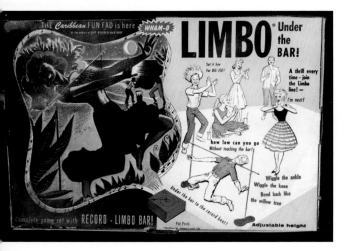

LIMBO
Wham-O 1961
$30 - $40

THREE CHIPMUNKS CROSS COUNTRY GAME
Hasbro 1959
Game series based on the David Seville singing sensations. Included ACORN HUNT and BIG RECORD.
$40 - $50

ELVIS PRESLEY GAME
Teenage Games 1957
Based on the King. The single most expensive game of the post-war era. Neat "Elvis" spinner.
$1500 - $1800

THREE CHIPMUNK BIG RECORD
Hasbro 1960
$50 - $55

THREE CHIPMUNKS ACORN HUNT
Hasbro 1960
$35 - $40

JACKSON FIVE ACTION GAME
Shindana Toys 1972
Jumbo card game based on the Motown singing group.
Courtesy of Rick Polizzi
$35 - $45

ELVIS PRESLEY KING OF ROCK
King of Rock Game Co.
1979
$55 - $65

BEN-HUR
Lowell 1959
Based on the MGM's "Mighty" production. Beautiful and rare game, with little plastic chariots.
$150 - $200

Inside of BEN-HUR

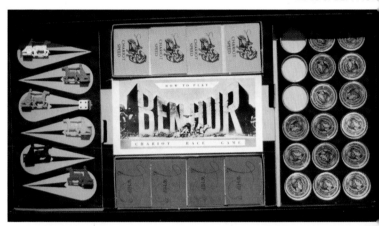

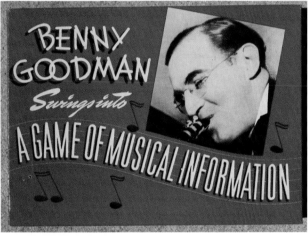

BENNY GOODMAN GAME OF MUSICAL INFORMATION
Toy Creations 1940s
Benny's beautiful game came complete with toy xylophone.
Courtesy of Rick Polizzi
$125 - $150

PECK'S BAD BOY
Milton Bradley 1939
"With the Circus." Based on the RKO movie starring Tommy Kelly. Game seems to be about sneaking into the circus. Another game, TOM SAWYER, was also based on a movie starring Kelly.
$55 - $65

CUGAT CANASTA BASQUETTE
Kuhlman Plastics 1950s
"Swing it and play... Cugat's way." Swing and Mambo maven Xavier Cugat lent his name to this plastic Canasta tray... "America's Finest."
$25 - $35

TOM SAWYER
Milton Bradley 1937
Based on David O. Selznick's movie starring Tommy Kelly.
$75 - $95

THE WIZARD OF OZ GAME
Cadaco 1974
"From the MGM Movie, an Annual Television Favorite."
$20 - $25

GAY PURR-EE
Whitman 1962
Based on the animated feature about an unescorted cat running around Paris.
$30 - $40

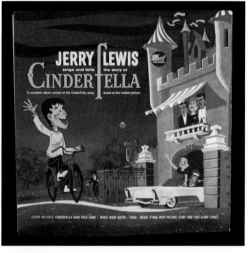

CINDERFELLA
Dot Records 1960
Based on movie starring Jerry Lewis. This was a record album with a game printed on the back.
Courtesy of Rick Polizzi
$50 - $75

BLADE RUNNER
CPC 1982
Highly sought after game based on the movie starring Harrison Ford.
$75 - $100

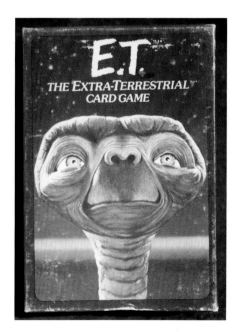

E.T. THE EXTRA-TERRESTRIAL CARD GAME
Parker Brothers 1982
Based on the movie. Full size game also available (see first book).
$10 - $15

THE THIEF OF BAGDAD
Selchow and Righter
1930s
Scare Junior Edition,
based on the movie.
*Courtesy of Jeff
Lowe's
ExtravaGAMEza*
$50 - $60

SHERLOCK HOLMES
National Games 1940
Based on the famous detective. Photo cover of actor Basil Rathbone.
$150 - $200

DOCTOR DOLITTLE
Mattel 1967
Based on the movie starring Rex Harrison. Based on
the 3-D game series which included BARBIE WORLD
OF FASHION, GENTLE BEN, and MAJOR MATT
MASON SPACE EXPLORATION GAME.
$55 - $75

THE LITTLE COLONEL
Selchow & Righter 1930
Although the game says it's based on the famous novel, it's obvious
it is Shirley Temple, who starred in the movie, on the cover.
$75 - $100

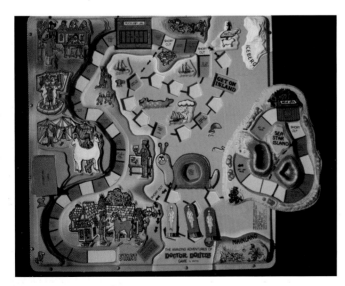

Inside of DOCTOR DOLITTLE.

DOCTOR DOLITTLE
Whitman 1967
Game-Pak Card Game based o
the movie. With "Plastilon"
plastic playing board sheet.
$25 - $34

ORD OF THE RINGS
ilton Bradley 1979
ased on the Ralph Baski's animated version of J.R.R. Tolkien's books.
5 - $35

THE DANCING PRINCESS
Hasbro 1962
$40 - $45

HE SINGING BONE
asbro 1962
ne of three games based on segments of the MGM film produc-
n of the *World of the Brother's Grimm*. Other games included
OBBLER AND THE ELVES and THE DANCING PRINCESS.
0 - $45

OUR GANG TIPPLE TOPPLE GAME
All-Fair 1930
Skill and action game in which cardboard cutouts of
"Our Gang" are knocked over to reveal points.
$250 - $350

OBBLER AND THE ELVES
asbro 1962
5 - $35

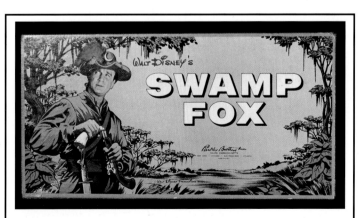

SWAMP FOX
Parker Brothers 1960
Based on the Disney TV show segments starring Leslie Nielsen.
$50 - $60

ANNETTE'S SECRET PASSAGE GAME
Parker Brothers 1958
Based on the star of the *Mickey Mouse Club*, Annette Funicello. Scarce game.
$75 - $100

WALT DISNEY'S CINDERELLA
Parker Brothers 1950
Based on the classic Disney film. Cinderella's glass slipper was an old MONOPOLY "shoe."
$55 - $75

WALT DISNEY'S CINDERELLA
Transogram 1960s
Small, simple card game.
$20 - $25

SNOW WHITE AND THE SEVEN DWARFS
Milton Bradley 1937
Based on the original Disney film. All kinds of neat wood pieces, including a wooden apple.
$150 - $200

Inside of SNOW WHITE AND THE SEVEN DWARFS.

WALT DISNEY'S 20,000 LEAGUES UNDER THE SEA
Jaymar Games 1954
Rare game based on the live action Disney film.
$55 - $75

WALT DISNEY'S 20,000 LEAGUES UNDER THE SEA
Gardner Games 1950s
$60 - $75

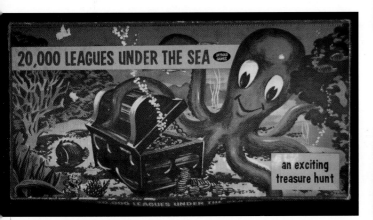

20,000 LEAGUES UNDER THE SEA
Jaymar Games 1950s
This version of the game came out after the Disney film had faded.
$20

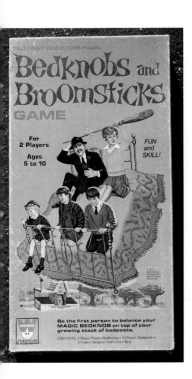

Left:
BEDKNOBS AND BROOM-STICKS
Whitman 1971
Based on the animated/live action Disney film starring Angela Lansbury.
$30 - $45

WALT DISNEY'S PETER PAN
Transogram 1953
Based on the film.
$45 - $55

WINNIE THE POOH HONEY TREE GAME
Ideal 1966
"Help Winnie the Pooh down from the honey tree."
Scarce game involving marbles and a honey tree.
Courtesy of Rick Polizzi
$55 - $75

WALT DISNEY SAFETY GAME
Parker Brothers 1963
Puzzle game, based on the TV show ("I'm no fool, no sir-ree, I'm going to live to be a hundred and three...").
$30 - $40

153

WALT DISNEY'S STEPS 'N' CHUTES
Transgram 1963
Mickey Mouse Club game of CHUTES AND LADDERS, based on re-runs.
$20 - $25

MICKEY MOUSE PICTURE MATCHING GAME
Parker Brothers 1950s
Bizarre, shoddy game by Parker Brothers. I'm not sure
if this belongs to a larger set of games.
$25 - $35

KLOMP-IT
Gaf 1972
Rare View-Master game. Came with two View-Master viewers. Players used
suction cupped wands to "Klomp" the Disney image they needed.
$40 - $50

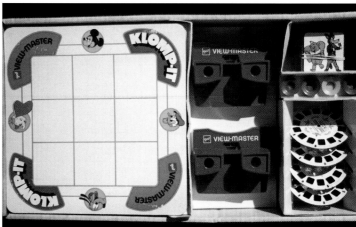

Inside of KLOMP-IT.

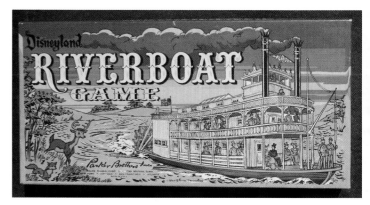

DISNEYLAND RIVERBOAT
Parker Brothers 1960
One of series of cheap games sold through the
Disneyland park in the 1950s (see first book).
$30 - $40

WALT DISNEY'S DONALD DUCK FLIPS HIS LID
Gardner Games 1950s
Similar to HATS OFF.
$40 - $50

WALT DISNEY'S DONALD DUCK'S PARTY GAME
Parker Brother 1938
$150 - $200

WALT DISNEY'S DONALD DUCK'S PARTY GAME
Parker Brothers 1938
Beautiful early Disney board game. Donald Duck figural spinner, Donald Duck moving pieces in different poses, and a great board showing Donald going through the paces. Object of the game is to collect three "prizes," all the time having to perform inane stunts like "recite your a-b-c's" or "meow like a kitty." The outside box cover apron has a continuous stream of Donald drawings going all around the perimeter. This game was re-issued in the 1950s.

DONALD DUCK BEAN BAG PARTY GAME
Parker Brothers 1939
Very large bean bag toss game.
$150 - $200

DONALD DUCK'S PARTY GAME
Parker Brothers 1950s
Reissue of earlier game.
$35 - $45

PICTURE THIS
Standard Toykraft 1963
Based on the CBS game show. Very rare game.
Courtesy of Matt Ottinger
$65 - $85

FACE THE FACTS
Lowell 1961
"Played exactly as played on the CBS Television Network." Wally Wood cover.
$50 - $65

TRUTH OR CONSEQUENCES
Gabriel 1955
$75 - $100

TRUTH OR CONSEQUENCES
Gabriel 1955
"The Funniest Party Game of All." Jack Bailey took over the game from Ralph Edwards when the show moved to NBC, and this home game is from that period. In this elaborate game, players are read a silly question from the "Truth" side of the wheel, and must answer. If they cannot, they pick a humiliating stunt from the "Consequences" side. And so on and so forth. Beautiful game.

TRUTH OR CONSEQUENCES
Lowell 1962
Rare version of the game by this company.
$55 - $75

GROUCHO'S YOU BET YOUR LIFE
Lowell 1955
Based on the NBC TV show featuring Groucho Marx. Came with a huge timer emblazoned with Groucho's face.
$75 - $100

GROUCHO TV QUIZ
Pressman 1954
$150 - $200

GROUCHO TV QUIZ
Pressman 1954
Gorgeous game based on the NBC TV game show starring Groucho Marx. It's a simple game, but very fun. You point the tiny plastic Groucho figure (complete with cigar) to the question, and when placed on the answer circle, points to the correct response. It's magic! Believe it or not, the game came with fake Groucho mustache, eyebrows, glasses, and cigar for the "M.C" to wear.

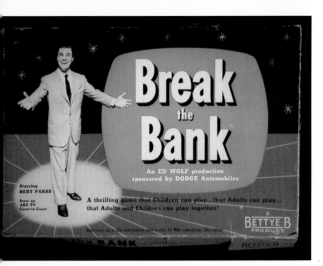

BREAK THE BANK
Bettye-B 1955
Based on the ABC TV show featuring Bert Parks. This is the
first edition of the game, with metal coins (see first book).
$5 - $75

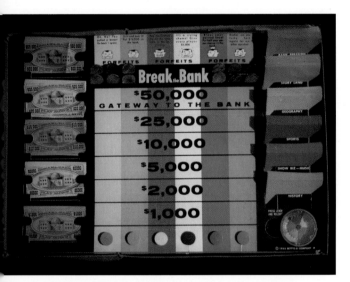

Inside of BREAK THE BANK.

YOUR SURPRISE PACKAGE
Ideal 1961
Based on the CBS TV show featuring players vying to
guess the contents of a "surprise package." Rare game.
$5 - $85

YOUR FIRST IMPRESSION
Lowell 1962
"Educational game based on the popular NBC Television Show."
$40 - $50

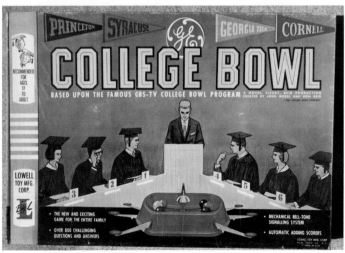

COLLEGE BOWL
Lowell 1962
Based on the "Famous CBS-TV College Bowl
Program." *JEOPARDY* for college students.
Courtesy of Rick Polizzi
$40 - $50

HOLLYWOOD SQUARES
Ideal 1974
2nd version of this NBC game show (see first book).
$20 - $25

DOUGH RE MI
Lowell 1960
Based on the NBC game show. This rare
and desirable game came with a toy xylophone to pound out the many tunes.
Courtesy of Matt Ottinger
$75 - $100

THE SKY'S THE LIMIT
Kohner 1955
Based on the NBC TV show featuring Gene Rayburn.
Very rare game had players performing hilarious stunts.
Courtesy of Matt Ottinger
$75 - $100

EVERYBODY'S TALKING!
Watkins-Strathmore Co. 1967
Based on the ABC TV game show.
$15 - $25

MISSING LINKS
Milton Bradley 1964
Proudly advertised as "The Game You See on Television."
$15 - $20

THE MATCH GAME
Milton Bradley 1963
Second Edition of the "Fun Packed TV Show" (see first book).
$15 - $20

SUPERMARKET SWEEP
Milton Bradley 1966
Courtesy of Matt Ottinger
$55 - $65

SUPERMARKET SWEEP
Milton Bradley 1966
Based on the TV show where contestants ran down supermarket aisles grabbing items. Players answer questions to win time to "power shop." Player with the biggest total "purchase" is the winner. Came with "Quick-Tick" Timer.

EAT THE CLOCK
owell 1957
ased on the TV game show of stunt hijinx. This game was
re-release of the earlier 1954 edition (see first book).
ourtesy of Rick Polizzi
35 - $45

BEAT THE CLOCK
Milton Bradley 1969
"New 2nd Edition." New version of the new version of the old game (see first book).
$15 - $20

YOURS FOR A SONG
Lowell 1961
Based on the ABC game show starring Bert Parks.
The game had players singing for their suppers.
$35 - $45

WINDOW SHOPPING
Lowell 1961
Based on the very rare TV game show game.
Courtesy of Matt Ottinger
$65 - $85

EDUCATIONAL CONCENTRATION
Milton Bradley 1964
Rare children's edition of the classic game show.
Courtesy of Matt Ottinger
$25 - $35

TWENTY ONE
Lowell 1956
$55 - $75

EDUCATIONAL PASSWORD
Milton Bradley 1962
Another rare children's edition.
$25 - $35

EDUCATIONAL PASSWORD
Milton Bradley 1970s
Another, later version of the children's edition.
Above two games courtesy of Matt Ottinger
$15 - $20

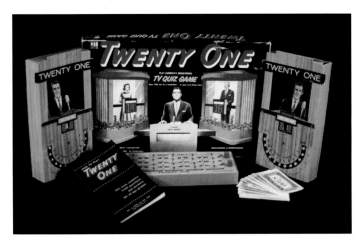

TWENTY ONE
Lowell 1956
Based on the NBC TV quiz game show that created the game show scandals of the 1950s. Beautifully made game included questions, answers, money, and two sound-proof booths, complete with contestants.

EYE GUESS
Milton Bradley 1969
Fourth and final edition of Bill Cullen's NBC TV game show (see first book).
$15 - $20

WHEEL OF FORTUNE TV GAME
Milton Bradley 1975
First game based on the popular TV show.
$10 - $15

BATTA HAI
Cadaco 1966
Box claims it's the "Home Edition of the Exciting TV Game." Domino style game. "Batta Hai" is what you cry when you win.
$25 - $35

THE GONG SHOW
American 1977
Yes, they even made a game from this abysmal show.
Courtesy of Rick Polizzi
$20 - $30

LET'S MAKE A DEAL
Milton Bradley 1964
Scarce first version of the NBC TV show.
$30 - $40

FAMILY FEUD
Milton Bradley 1979
Fifth edition of popular TV show.
$5 - $8

ALUMNI FUN
Milton Bradley 1964
Trivia game "As Seen on TV."
$15 - $25

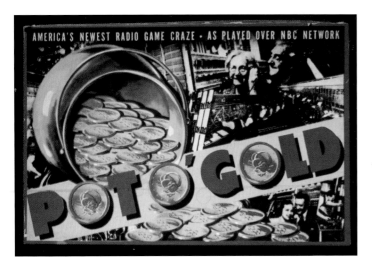

POT O' GOLD
Toy Creation 1940
Based on the NBC radio program. Basically a bingo game, as players vie to have their "exchange" numbers rolled on the special dice, and eventually "dial" their number.
$75 - $100

VOX POP
Milton Bradley 1938
Original edition of the game. Game utensils for this game are identical to PAUL WING'S SPELLING BEE.
Courtesy of Matt Ottinger
$30 - $40

Inside of POT O' GOLD.

PAUL WING'S SPELLING BEE
Milton Bradley 1938
Based on the radio show. One of the first "game shows" in any sense. Rare game.
$75 - $100

VOX POP
Milton Bradley 1938
Second version of "Radio's Most Popular Quiz-Game."
Courtesy of Matt Ottinger
$30 - $40

Inside of PAUL WING'S SPELLING BEE.

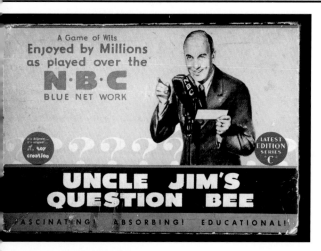

UNCLE JIM'S QUESTION BEE
y Creations 1938
ong with PAUL WING'S SPELLING BEE, one of
e first game shows. "Latest Edition, Series C."
0 - $50

CAPTAIN KANGAROO PARADE AROUND THE TREASURE HOUSE
Transogram 1970
$25 - $35

AKE IT OR LEAVE IT!
ndine 1942
ed on the radio game from a rare game company.
is is the original "$64 question" program.
0 - $40

WHO AM I?
Ed-U-Cards 1954
Based on children's show host, Pinky Lee. Neat cut out masks.
$50 - $75

PTAIN KANGAROO
ton Bradley 1956
ed on the CBS children's show. Beautiful board and playing pieces.
$ - $65

PINKY LEE AND THE RUNAWAY FRANKFURTHERS
Lisbeth-Whiting 1954
Cool miniature weiners!
Courtesy of Rick Polizzi
$55 - $65

PINKY LEE GAME TIME
Pressman 1955
Everything you needed for a fun time!
$55 - $65

LAUREL AND HARDY
Transogram 1962
Based on the animated series by *Bozo The Clown* Larry Harmon.
$75 - $100

MAGIC MIDWAY
Cadaco 1962
Based on the NBC children's TV show. Cool Midway "tickets."
$30 - $40

WOODY WOODPECKER'S UP THE TREE
Whitman 1967
One of many games based on the Walter Lantz character.
$25 - $30

DIVER DAN TUG-O-WAR GAME
Milton Bradley 1961
Based on the Saturday morning TV show.
Courtesy of Rick Polizzi
$40 - $55

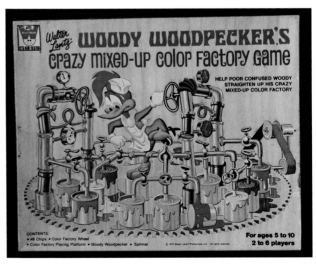

**WOODY WOODPECKER'S CRAZY
MIXED-UP COLOR FACTORY**
Whitman 1972
"Help poor confused Woody straighten up his
crazy mixed-up color factory." Obscure game.
$30 - $40

LOONEY TUNES GAME
Milton Bradley 1968
Based on the Warner Brothers characters.
Courtesy of Rick Polizzi
$45 - $55

DOLLY AND DANIEL WHALE
Milton Bradley 1963
Based on an obscure TV cartoon.
$40 - $50

BUGS BUNNY ADVENTURE GAME
Milton Bradley 1961
Early Bugs game. Great cover.
$35 - $45

HECTOR HEATHCOTE
Transogram 1963
$150 - $200

FELIX THE CAT
Milton Bradley 1960
Beautiful game board based on the revived animated cartoon of the famous cat and his bag of "magic tricks."
$30 - $40

HECTOR HEATHCOTE
Transogram 1963
"The Minute-And-A-Half Man." Based on the NBC Saturday morning cartoon show starring Hector, Hasimoto-San (The Japanese House Mouse), and Silly Sidney (the Absent-Minded Elephant). Game included neat Hector figural pieces as well as a "Cannon" bowling device. Magilla Gorilla made his debut on this show.

TWINKLES GAME
Milton Bradley 1961
"His Trip to the Star Factory." Rare game based on Twinkles,
the first original cereal character to have a board game.
Courtesy of Rick Polizzi
$150 - $175

HOPPITY HOOPER
Milton Bradley 1964
Based on the creator Jay Ward's (*Rocky and Bullwinkle*) TV show.
$75 - $95

HIGH SPIRITS WITH CALVIN AND THE COLONEL
Milton Bradley 1962
Based on the TV cartoon, which itself was based on *AMOS N' ANDY*.
This is premiere game designer Sid Sackson's first game.
$55 - $75

ROCKY AND HIS FRIENDS
Milton Bradley 1960
First game based on the famous Jay Ward creations. Cover
features other characters such as Sherman and Mr. Peabody,
and rare shots of Gidney and Lloyd, the Moon Men.
$75 - $100

BULLWINKLE TRAVEL ADVENTURE
Transogram 1970
Rare game.
$50 - $75

WENDY THE GOOD LITTLE WITCH
Milton Bradley 1966
Rare companion game to CASPER (see first book). Kind of
a Backgammon game in which players tried to move all
four of their "witch's hats" from start to finish.
$175 - $200

CASPER THE FRIENDLY GHOST FUN BOX
Saalfield 1966
Based on the Harveytoon animated character. This activity set included books, stand-up figures, stencil art ... and a board game, which included figural pieces of Casper and Spooky, the "tuff little ghost."
$75 - $100

KING LEONARDO
Milton Bradley 1960
Based on the animated TV show starring the King and his Subjects. Cards were filled with pictures of characters from the show.
$55 - $75

TERRYTOONS HIDE N' SEEK GAME
Transogram 1960
Based on the popular Terrytoon animated characters. Every obscure character you can think of is on the cover, including Tom Terrific.
Courtesy of Rick Polizzi
$75 - $100

DEPUTY DAWG
Milton Bradley 1960
Based on the NBC animated TV show. *Deputy Dawg* originally appeared in theaters.
$55 - $75

DEPUTY DAWG TV LOTTO
Ideal 1961
Series included TERRYTOONS TV LOTTO.
$35 - $45

TERRYTOONS POP-OUTS
Ideal 1961
Bingo variant involving picture puzzles of Dinky Duck, Goose and Gander, Heckle and Jeckle, and Mighty Mouse. One of the variations allows a player to be "official spinner" during the game. Whoopee!
$40 - $50

THE SIMPSONS 3-D CHESS
Unknown 1992
Super neat plastic figural pieces of the family.
$35 - $45

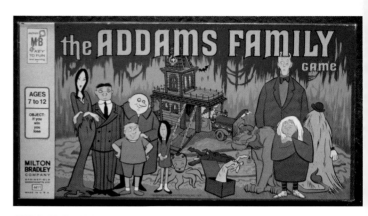

ADDAMS FAMILY
Milton Bradley 1974
Based on the NBC animated cartoon series, which was based on the
TV show, which was based on Charles Addams' drawings.
$30 - $40

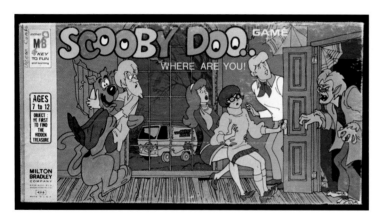

SCOOBY DOO
Milton Bradley 1973
"Where are you?" Based on the popular animated
TV show about the cowardly Great Dane.
$30 - $40

FAT ALBERT AND THE COSBY KIDS
Milton Bradley 1973
Based on the cartoon, which was based on
a comedy routine by Bill Cosby.
Courtesy of Rick Polizzi
$25 - $35

FUNKY PHANTOM
Milton Bradley 1971
Based on the obscure animated TV series.
$30 - $40

TOM AND JERRY
Milton Bradley 1948
$75 - $100

TOM AND JERRY
Milton Bradley 1948
"Gay Double Feature Cartoon Game." First game made about MGM's famous cartoon cat and mouse. Cute plastic mouse and cat pieces were moved by separate Tom and Jerry spinners. Beautifully drawn box cover and board. Since the duo are known for trying to kill each other in horrible ways, it's interesting to note that the game is "Psych-Tested." I guess they had different standards back then.

MR. MAGOO GAME
Standard Toykraft 1964
Based on the NBC animated series.
$55 -$75

TOM AND JERRY ADVENTURES IN BLUNDERLAND
Transogram 1965
Based on the mouse and cat's romp through a "wonderland."
$60 - $75

OH MAGOO YOU'VE DONE IT AGAIN!
Warren 1978
Based on the CBS TV series.
$25 - $35

MISTER MAGOO VISITS THE ZOO
Lowell 1961
First game based on the Jim Backus voiced theatrical cartoon character.
$75 - $100

Right:
TALK TO CECIL
Mattel 1961
$85 - $110

TALK TO CECIL
Mattel 1961
Based on the Bob Clampett characters which first appeared on the ABC animated series *Matty's Funday Funnies*, about a boy and his sea-sick sea serpent, Cecil. The amazing game included small plastic "Beany" moving pieces, a huge Cecil "puzzle path" game board, and a Talking Cecil hand-puppet, which told players where and how to move. Others games from this time included JUMPING DJ SURPRISE ACTION GAME and BEANY AND CECIL MATCH-IT GAME (see first book).

RUFF AND REDDY
Transogram 1962
Based on the first NBC animated series. This was Hanna-Barbera's first animated creation.
$55 - $75

HOPPY THE HOPPAROO
Transogram 1965
Very scarce game based on an obscure character from *The Flintstones* animated show.
$150 - $200

LIPPY THE LION FLIPS GAME
Transogram 1962
"With Hardy Har-Har the Laughless Hyena." Rare game based on TV animated show.
$100 - $125

YOGI BEAR GO FLY A KITE GAME
Transogram 1961
"Fascinating Game of Perception." Based on the animated TV series. Cover shows scarce characters, including his girlfriend Cindy Bear.
$75 - $100

MUSHMOUSE AND PUNKIN' PUSS
Ideal 1964
Obscure game based on animated segments that first appeared on ABC's *THE MAGILLA GORILLA SHOW*. Hillbilly feudin' game.
$150 - $200

Inside of MUSHMOUSE AND PUNKIN' PUSS.

PETER POTAMUS
Ideal 1964
"Based on the popular TV series." Very rare game which continued the adventures of the purple hippo and his assistant So-So.
$300 - $400

RICOCHET RABBIT & DROOP-A-LONG COYOTE
Ideal 1964
Another game based on animated segments that got their start on *THE MAGILLA GORILLA SHOW*.
$250 - $300

MAGILLA GORILLA
Ideal 1964
Based on the ABC animated TV series. Game involves players trying to escape from pet store owner Mr. Peebles.
$250 - $350

TOUCHÉ TURTLE
Transogram 1962
The original hero in a half-shell. Based on the animated segments first seen on the *WALLY GATOR* show.
$150 - $200

HUCKLEBERRY HOUND WESTERN GAME
Milton Bradley 1959
"Exciting but simple game." Track game based on the early Hanna-Barbera animated series. Board includes graphics of other early characters, including Pixie and Dixie, Mr. Jinx, and an early Yogi Bear.
$35 - $45

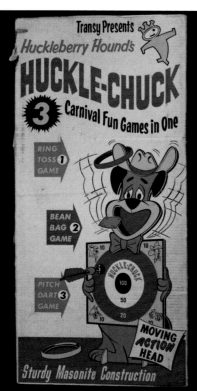

Left:
HUCKLE-CHUCK
Transogram 1961
Huckleberry Hound game. "3
Carnival Fun Games in One."
Kids threw darts, rings, and
bean bags at a large wood
image of the happy hound.
$55 - $75

ATOM ANT
Transogram 1966
"Saves the Day Game." Based on the NBC
animated series about the diminutive hero.
$150 - $200

TOP CAT
Whitman 1962
Based on the ABC TV ani-
mated series (which appeared
in prime time). Very rare
game in which Top Cat and
his cronies attempt to canvas
the neighborhood, pick up
items (like fish), outwit
Officer Dribble, and arrive at
Top Cat's trash can.
$175 - $225

CRUSADER RABBIT TV GAME
Tryne Sales 1956
$250 - $350

CRUSADER RABBIT TV GAME
Tryne Sales 1956
Extremely rare game based on the first animated cartoon character created by
Jay Ward expressly for television. Although the game is simple, and involves
players hunting for pieces of a puzzle to complete a picture of Crusader Rabbit,
it is well made and extremely colorful. The spinner is a portrait of Rags the
tiger, and the color indicating the player's move is shown in his right eye.

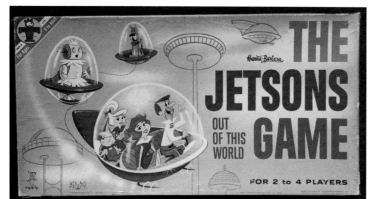

THE JETSONS OUT OF THIS WORLD GAME
Transogram 1962
Based on the ABC prime time animated series. Playing pieces included the whole
family (including Rosie the Robot), as well as plastic space ships and comets.
$150 - $200

MIGHTY MOUSE PLAYHOUSE RESCUE GAME
Harett-Gilmar 1956
Based on the popular CBS Terrytoon animated series. Lots of characters on the box cover.
Courtesy of Jeff Lowe's ExtravaGAMEza
$5 - $75

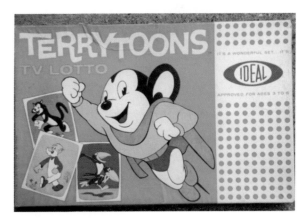

TERRYTOONS TV LOTTO
Ideal 1961
Courtesy of Jeff Lowe's ExtravaGAMEza
$30 - $45

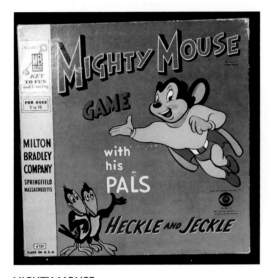

MIGHTY MOUSE
Milton Bradley 1957
"With his Pals Heckle and Jeckle."
$60 - $75

SPACE ANGEL
Transogram 1965
Based on the animated TV series.
$100 - $150

TERRYTOONS MIGHTY MOUSE
Milton Bradley 1978
$5 - $35

STAR TREK
Hasbro 1974
Based on the NBC animated series
which utilized the original cast's voices.
$50 - $75

JONNY QUEST CARD GAME
Milton Bradley 1964
Card game based on the super cool animated TV series. There is
an extremely rare full size game as well (see first book).
$100 - $150

UNDERDOG BUILD THE TALLEST BUILDING
Whitman 1973
Scarce game involving building buildings.
$30 - $40

GEORGE OF THE JUNGLE
Parker Brothers 1968
Based on Jay Ward's animated TV show. The object was to get
George safely through the perils of the jungle and back to his "hut."
$100 - $150

CAPTAIN QUANTUM VS. THE UGLY DRUGGIES
Play To Win, Inc. 1990
Public Service game from the creators of Ren and Stimpy. I was told this was
a prototype for a game that was never produced. May just be a promo.
$100 - $150

UNDERDOG
Milton Bradley 1964
Based on the NBC animated series starring the voice of Wally Cox. Beautiful cover.
$50 - $75

Index

20,000 LEAGUES UNDER THE SEA, 153
20,000 LEAGUES UNDER THE SEA, WALT DISNEY'S, 153
3 BLIND MICE, 71
3 STOOGES FUN HOUSE GAME, THE, 143
4 ALARM, 94
9-ALL, 64
ADDAMS FAMILY GAME, THE, 168
AFRICAN ANIMAL HUNT, 111
AGGRAVATION, 65
AIR MAIL PILOT, 113
AIR TRIX, 81
AIRPORT, 22
ALI BABA AND THE FORTY THIEVES, 134
ALICE IN WONDERLAND, 134
ALL STAR FOOTBALL, 26
ALL-PRO BASEBALL, OFFICIAL, 29
ALL-PRO BASKETBALL, OFFICIAL, 32
ALUMNI FUN, 161
AMAZE, 100
AMERICAN DREAM, THE, 20
AND THEN THERE WERE NONE, 133
ANGELA CARTWRIGHT BUTTONS' N BOWS GAME, 129
ANIMAL TWISTER, 72
ANNIE OAKLEY, 7
AQUAMAN GAME, JUSTICE LEAGUE OF AMERICA, 137
AQUANAUTS, 125
ARMAGEDDON, 114
ARREST AND TRIAL, 126
ASTRO LAUNCH, 69
ATOM ANT SAVES THE DAY GAME, 172
AUCTION, 23
AUCTION TRIPOLEY, 60
AUTO DROME, 34
AUTOFUN, 103
AVALANCHE, 85

BABAR AND HIS FRIENDS SEE-SAW GAME, 135
BABYSITTER, 75
BACKGAMMON, 22
BACKGAMMON-PARCHEESI COMBINATION, THE NEW, 64
BALDICER, 112
BALI, 63
BANDERSNATCH, 74
BARBIE MISS LIVELY LIVIN' GAME, 139
BARBIE WORLD OF FASHION GAME, THE, 139
BARK N' BITE, 72
BARNEY MILLER, 129
BARNSTORMER, 82
BARREL OF MONKEYS, 79
BAS-KET, 30
BASEBALL, 29
BASKETBALL, SAMSONITE, 31
BATMAN AND ROBIN GAME, 138
BATMAN CARD GAME, 137
BATMAN JIGSAW PUZZLE GAME, THE, 138
BATS IN YOUR BELFRY, 67
BATTA HAI, 161
BATTLESHIP, 11
BEACHHEAD INVASION, 11
BEAT THE BUZZ, 116
BEAT THE CLOCK GAME, 159
BEAT THE CLOCK, NEW, 159
BEDNOBS AND BROOMSTICKS GAME, 153
BEETLE, 51
BELIEVE IT OR NOT! GAME, RIPLEY'S, 146
BEN-HUR, 148
BENNY GOODMAN SWINGS INTO A GAME OF MUSICAL INFORMATION, 148
BID & BLUFF, 23

BIG BOARD, THE, 18
BIG JOHN, 114
BIG THUMB, 83
BIG TOWN NEWS REPORTING & PRINTING GAME, 127
BIG WIG, 120
BILLBOARD, 101
BILLY BLASTOFF SPACE GAME, 138
BIRD BRAIN, 71
BIRD WATCHER, THE GAME OF, 93
BIRDIE GOLF, 36
BIZERTE GERTIE, 12
BLACK COMMUNITY GAME, THE, 104
BLADE RUNNER, 149
BLONDIE GAME, THE, 132
BLOOD FLOW GAME, THE, 116
BOBBIN NOGGIN, 77
BODY LANGUAGE, 144
BOMB THE NAVY, 11
BOMBER BALL, 11
BONANZA, 8
BOOB TUBE RACE GAME, 81
BOONDOGGLE, 120
BOP BASEBALL, 48
BOP THE BEETLE, 75
BOWL BOUND, 27
BOWLING CARD GAME, 35
BOZO THE CLOWN CIRCUS GAME, 142
BOZO THE CLOWN IN CIRCUS-LAND, 143
BREAK THE BANK, 157
BREAKER 19, 103
BRIDG-IT, 84
BRIDG-IT, ADVANCED, 84
BROADSIDES & BOARDING PARTIES, 14
BROADWAY HANDICAP, 30
BUCCANEERS, THE, 15
BUFFALO BILL JR'S CATTLE ROUND-UP GAME, 7
BUG, 51
BUG BOPPER, 78
BUGALOOS, 130
BUGS BUNNY ADVENTURE GAME, 165
BUILDING BOOM!, 104
BULLS AND BEARS, 18
BULLWINKLE TRAVEL ADVENTURE, 166
BUMPBACK, 105
BUMPY THE FUNNY LITTLE BEAR, 91
BUNCO, 59
BUNNY RABBIT, 91
BURKE'S LAW, 126
BUSY BEE, 51
BUY AND SELL, 19

CAGEY MONKEY GAME, THE, 76
CAMELOT, 14
CAMMY, 105
CANASTA, 59
CANDYLAND, 96
CAMPBELL KIDS SHOPPING GAME, THE, 141
CAPTAIN AMERICA GAME, 135
CAPTAIN KANGAROO PARADE AROUND THE TREASURE HOUSE GAME, 163
CAPTAIN KANGAROO, THE GAME OF, 163
CAPTAIN QUANTUM VS. THE UGLY DRUGGIES, 174
CAREFUL, 75
CARTEL, 21
CASPER THE FRIENDLY GHOST FUN BOX, 167
CASPER THE FRIENDLY GHOST GAME, 55
CAT AND MOUSE, GAME OF, 70
CATCH 'EM, 70
CATCH A CHICKEN TORIE, 13
CATHEDRAL, 114
CENTRAL BANK, 19

CHAIRMAN OF THE BOARD, 21
CHALLENGE FOOTBALL, 23
CHAMPIONSHIP FIGHT GAME, 31
CHARADES, 71
CHARLIE AND THE CHOCOLATE FACTORY, 133
CHARLOTTE'S WEB GAME, 135
CHEQUERO, 64
CHERRY PIE FUN GAME, 71
CHESS, 22
CHICLETS GUM VILLAGE GAME, 140
CHIPPENDALES AFTER HOURS GAME, 142
CHIPS, 126
CHITTY CHITTY BANG BANG ELECTRIC QUIZ GAME, 46
CHONCA, 111
CHUG-A-LUG, 116
CINDERELLA GAME, WALT DISNEY'S, 152
CIRCULATION, 116
CIRCUS BOY, 129
CIRCUS GAME, EMMETT KELLY'S, 143
CLAIROL BEAUTY GAME, THE, 141
CLIMB THE MOUNTAIN, 94
CLIPPER RACE, 31
CLOCK-A-GAME, 90
CLOWN CAPERS, 94
CLUEDO, 58
CLUNK-A-GLUNK, 82
COBBLER AND THE ELVES, THE, 151
COCKY COMPASS, 100
COLLEGE BOWL, 157
COLLEGE FOOTBALL, SPORTS ILLUSTRATED, 27
COLLISION!, 32
COLORATION, 118
COMBINATION DICE GAME, 48
COMBINATION GAME SET, 65
COMEDY CENTRAL INDECISION 96, 146
COMIN' ROUND THE MOUNTAIN, ELECTRIC, 93
CONQUEROR CHESS, 65
CONQUEST OF THE RING, 115
CONTIGO, 23
COOTIE, 50
COOTIE HOUSE, 50
CORKY CLOWN BIG TOP CIRCUS GAME, 94
CORNER THE MARKET, 19
COUNT DOWN, 68
COWBOYS & INDIANS, GAME OF, 10
CRAZY FARM, 112
CRAZY MIXED-UP COLOR FACTORY GAME, WALTER LANTZ WOODY WOODPECKER'S, 164
CRIBBAGE, HOYLE OFFICIAL, 61
CROSS PURPOSES, 105
CROW, 59
CRUDE, 24
CRUSADE, 146
CRUSADER RABBIT GAME, 172
CUGAT CANASTA BASQUETTE, 148

DAI JOBI, 100
DANA GIRLS GAME, THE, 135
DANCING PRINCESS, THE, 151
DAVY CROCKETT ADVENTURES, WALT DISNEY'S, 6
DEALER MCDOPE DEALING GAME, 116
DEPUTY DAWG, 167
DEPUTY DAWG TV LOTTO, 167
DEPUTY, THE, 8
DETECTIVES, THE, 126
DETOUR, 104
DIAL, 117
DIAL 'N SPELL, 87
DICK TRACY SUPER DETECTIVE MYSTERY CARD GAME, 132

DICTATOR, 13
DISCOVERY, 146
DISNEYLAND RIVERBOAT GAME, 154
DIVER DAN TUG-O-WAR GAME, 164
DOBBIN DERBY, 109
DOCTOR DOLITTLE, 150
DOCTOR DOOLITTLE GAME-PAK CARD GAME, 150
DOLLY AND DANIEL WHALE GAME, 165
DON'T BREAK THE ICE, 56
DON'T BUG ME, 71
DON'T CATCH A COLD, 92
DON'T DUMP THE DAISY, 85
DON'T MISS THE BOAT!, 96
DON'T SPILL THE BEANS, 53
DONALD DUCK BEAN BAG PARTY GAME, WALT DISNEY'S, 155
DONALD DUCK FLIPS HIS LID GAME, WALT DISNEY'S, 154
DONALD DUCK'S PARTY GAME, WALT DISNEY'S, 155
DONDI FINDERS KEEPERS GAME, 131
DONDI PRAIRIE RACE GAME, 131
DONNY & MARIE OSMOND TV SHOW GAME, 130
DOUBLE OR NOTHIN', 43
DOUBLE SOME 'R' SET, 59
DOUBLETRACK, 105
DOUGH RE MI, 158
DOVER PATROL, 11
DOWN THE HATCH!, 107
DR. LIVINGSTONE, I PRESUME?, 111
DREAM DATE, 97
DRIVE-IN, 19
DRIVER TRAINING GAMES, 103
DROP IN THE BUCKET, 95
DUNCE, 53
DUNGEONS & DRAGONS, 145

E.T. THE EXTRA-TERRESTRIAL CARD GAME, 149
EARTH SATELLITE, 69
EASY MONEY, 19
EAT AT RALPH'S, 114
EDUCATIONAL CONCENTRATION, 160
EDUCATIONAL PASSWORD, 160
ELECTRO-DICE, RADIO SHACK, 62
ELECTROMATIC DIAL QUIZ, 121
ELECTRON-O-BRAIN, THE, 122
ELLA CINDERS, 132
ELSIE AND HER FAMILY, 141
ELVIS PRESLEY GAME, THE, 147
ELVIS PRESLEY KING OF ROCK GAME, 148
ENSIGN O'TOOLE U.S.S. APPLEBY GAME, 16
ESCORT, 97
ESP, 23
ESPIONAGE, THE GAME OF, 88
EVADE, 25
EVENTS, 23
EVERYBODY'S TALKING!, 158
EXPANSE, 20
EXPLORING, 146
EYE GUESS, 160

F-TROOP MINI-BOARD CARD GAME, 9
FACE THE FACTS, 155
FAIRY TALE GAME, THE, 99
FAMILY AFFAIR, 46
FAMILY AFFAIR "WHERE'S MRS. BEASLEY?" GAME, THE, 128
FAMILY FEUD, 161
FANG BANG, 75
FARM MANAGEMENT, 112
FASCINATION, 44

FASCINATION CHECKERS, 44
FASCINATION POOL, 45
FAT ALBERT AND THE COSBY KIDS GAME, THE, 168
FAT BOY'S GAME, ELMER WHEELER'S, 135
FELIX THE CAT GAME, 165
FESS PARKER WILDERNESS TRAIL CARD GAME, 7
FINANCE, 20
FINDER'S KEEPERS, 84
FINGER DINGER MAN, 83
FINGERS HARRY, 88
FIRE CHIEF, 98
FIRE HOUSE MOUSE, 78
FIREBALL XL5, 123
FLAG GAME, THE GREAT AMERICAN, 119, 120
FLAPJACK, 42
FLASH GAME, JUSTICE LEAGUE OF AMERICA, THE, 137
FLATSY GAME, THE, 139
FLEA CIRCUS, 89
FLINCH, 58
FLIP & FLOP, 118
FLIP-IT TWENTY ONE, 144
FLYING ACES, 12
FLYING SAUCER HORSESHOE GAME, WHAM-O, 34
FLYING THE BEAM, 113
FOCUS, 64
FOIL, 25
FOOBA-ROU FOOTBALL, 26
FOOTBALL, 27
FOUR LANE ROAD RACING, 33
FREDDIE FROG, GAME OF, 92
FREEWAY, 102
FROGGER, 131
FRONT PAGE, 118
FRUSTRATION BALL, 45
FUGITIVE, THE, 125
FUN HOUSE, 95
FUN ON THE FARM, 112
FUNKY PHANTOM GAME, THE, 168
FUNNY FINGER, 72

G.I. JOE NAVY FROGMAN! GAME, 139
GALLOPING GOLF, 35
GARRISON'S GORILLAS, 16
GAY PURR-EE GAME, 149
GENTLE BEN ANIMAL HUNT, 128
GEORGE OF THE JUNGLE GAME, 174
GET IN THAT TUB, 86
GHOST, WORD GAME OF, 67
GIANT COOTIE, 49
GIANT STEP, 109
GIANT STEPS, 109
GIANT WHEEL COWBOYS AND INDIANS, 41
GIANT WHEEL PICTURE BINGO, 41
GIANT WHEEL THRILLS' N SPILLS HORSE RACE GAME, 40
GIDGET, 128
GIGGLE POOL, 73
GIGGLE STICK, 79
GINGERBREAD MAN, 99
GLOBE-TROTTERS, 101
GNIP GNOP, 78
GO, 22
GO GIN, 61
GO TO THE HEAD OF THE CLASS, 86
GOLF BY THE RULES, 37
GOLF GAME, LIGHT HORSE HARRY COOPER'S, 36
GOLFERINO, 37
GONG SHOW GAME, THE, 161
GOVERNMENT, 121
GRAY GHOST, THE, 15
GREEN GOBLIN, 63
GREEN HORNET QUICK SWITCH GAME, THE, 126
GRIZZLY ADAMS, 128
GROUCHO TV QUIZ, 156
GUESS AGAIN, 122
GUESS' N BEE, 52
GUNFIGHT AT O.K. CORRAL, 10

HANK AARON BASEBALL, 28
HAPPINESS, 89
HAPPY BIRTHDAY SURPRISE GAME, 84
HAPPY FACE, 78
HAPPY HOOKER GAME, XAVIERA'S, 142
HAPPY LANDING, 63
HAPPY, HAPPY BIRTHDAY GAME, 83
HARDY BOYS MYSTERY GAME, THE, 130
HARDY BOYS TREASURE GAME, 135
HAUNTED HOUSE, 67

HAVE-A-HEART, 55
HAWAII FIVE-O, 47
HEARTS, 61
HECTOR HEATHCOTE GAME, 165
HEE HAW, 112
HEIDI ELEVATOR GAME, 46
HEX, 99
HEY PA! THERE'S A GOAT ON THE ROOF, 84
HEY, FATSO, 86
HI-Q, DOUBLE GIANT, 66
HIGGLY PIGGLY, 106
HIGH SPIRITS, GAME OF, 166
HIGH STAKES, 80
HIGH-BID, 24
HIGHWAY PATROL, 126
HIGHWAY TRAFFIC, 102
HILLBILLIES COMIN' ROUND THE MOUNTAIN GAME, 93
HIPPOPOTAMUS, 45
HISPANIOLA, THE GAME OF, 53
HOC-KEY, 30
HOCUS POCUS, 77
HOGAN'S HEROES, 12
HOLLYWOOD AWARDS, 110
HOLLYWOOD GO, 110
HOLLYWOOD SQUARES TV GAME, THE, 158
HOME GAME, 146
HOME GOLF, 34
HONEY WEST, 125
HOOKEY, 108
HOP' N STOMP, 82
HOPPITY, 92
HOPPITY HOOPER GAME, 166
HOPPY THE HOPPAROO GAME, 170
HORSE PLAY, 54
HOT DIGGITY DOG, 73
HOT POTATO, 42
HOT ROD, 39
HUCK FINN, 130
HUCKLE-CHUCK, HUCKLEBERRY HOUND'S, 172
HUCKLEBERRY HOUND WESTERN GAME, 171
HUGGIN' THE RAIL, 33
HULK SMASH-UP ACTION GAME, THE INCREDIBLE, 138
HUMPTY DUMPTY, 55
HURRY WAITER!, 73

I WISH I WERE, 97
ICE CREAM GAME, 94
ICE CUBE, 92
IMPOSSIBLE GAME, THE, 115
IN PURSUIT OF PAR, 36
INSTANT REPLAY, JERRY KRAMER'S, 27
INTERSECTION, 104
IRONSIDE, 125
IT'S ABOUT TIME, 128

JACK AND THE BEANSTALK, 53
JACK NICKLAUS PRACTICE MAT, 36
JACK-BE-NIMBLE, 71
JACKSON FIVE ACTION GAME, 147
JALOPY RACE, 91
JATI, 22
JEEP BOARD, THE, 13
JERRY LEWIS CINDERFELLA, 149
JESSE JAMES, THE LEGEND OF, 7
JETSONS OUT OF THIS WORLD GAME, THE, 172
JIM PRENTICE ELECTRIC BASKETBALL, 32
JOCKEY, 30
JOHNNY CAN READ!, 87
JOHNNY ON THE PONY, 44
JOHNNY UNITAS FOOTBALL, 28
JOLLY ROGER, 106
JONATHAN LIVINGSTON SEAGULL, 133
JONNY QUEST CARD GAME, 174
JOURNEY TO THE UNKNOWN, 47
JUNIOR TABLE TOP BOWLING ALLEY, 35

KAPU, 59
KAR-ZOOM, 33
KARATE, THE GAME OF, 119
KEEP ON TRUCKIN', AMERICA, THE GAME OF, 103
KENTUCKY JONES HORSE AUCTION GAME, 128
KICK THE CAN, 43
KING LEONARDO AND HIS SUBJECTS GAME, 167
KING OF THE CHEESE, 70
KING OF THE HILL, 54
KISMET, THE GAME OF, 61
KLOMP-IT, 154
KNOCK-OFF!, 82

KOO KOO CHOO CHOO, 85
KOOKIE CHICKS, 77
KOOKY CARNIVAL, 95

LANCER, 48
LAND OF THE GIANTS, 124
LANDMARKS, THE GAME OF, 100
LASSIE, ADVENTURES OF, 127
LAUREL AND HARDY GAME, 164
LE MANS, 33
LEAP FROG, 74
LET'S FACE IT!, 87
LET'S FURNISH A HOUSE, 104
LET'S MAKE A DEAL, 161
LET'S TAKE A TRIP, 101
LEVERAGE, 105
LIEUTENANT, THE, 15
LIL SQUIRT, 56
LIMBO, 147
LIMBO, CHUBBY CHECKER, 147
LIPPY THE LION FLIPS GAME, 170
LITTLE BLACK SAMBO, 142
LITTLE CHIEF, 10
LITTLE COLONEL, THE, 150
LITTLE LEAGUE BASEBALL, APPROVED, 29
LITTLE ORPHAN ANNIE PURSUIT GAME, 132
LITTLE RED SCHOOL HOUSE, 86
LOLLI-POP LANE, 95
LONDON BRIDGE, 55
LONG SHOT, 29
LOONEY TUNES GAME, 165
LORD OF THE RINGS, THE, 151
LOST IN SPACE 3D ACTION FUN GAME, 46
LOST LITTLE PIGS, GAME OF, 99
LOST TREASURE, 96
LOVE BOAT, THE, 129
LUCKY BEE AND JOHNNY APPLESEED PRESCHOOL GAME BOX, 87
LUCKY CATCH, 93
LUCKY LOOPY, 109
LUCKY TOWN, 104
LUNAR LANDING GAME, LAY'S, 68

MACDONALD'S FARM GAME, 112
MAGIC MIDWAY GAME, 164
MAGIC ROBOT QUIZ GAME, 117
MAGIC THE GATHERING, 114
MAGIC! MAGIC! MAGIC!, 48
MAGILLA GORILLA GAME, 171
MAH-JONG, 66
MAJOR MATT MASON SPACE EXPLORATION GAME, 139
MATCH GAME, THE, 158
MEAN JOE GREENE FOOTBALL, 27
MECHANIC MAC, 98
MEET THE PRESIDENTS, 120
MELVIN THE MOON MAN, 42
MERRY CIRCUS GAME, THE, 91
MICHIGAN RUMMY, 60
MICKEY MONK, GAME OF, 92
MICKEY MOUSE PICTURE MATCHING GAME, 154
MIGHTY COMICS SUPER HEROES GAME, 136
MIGHTY HEROES ON THE SCENE GAME, 136
MIGHTY MOUSE GAME WITH HIS PALS HECKLE AND JECKLE, 173
MIGHTY MOUSE GAME, TERRYTOONS, 173
MIGHTY MOUSE PLAYHOUSE RESCUE GAME, TERRYTOON'S, 173
MILL GAME, SCHAPER'S, 52
MILL GAME, THE, 51
MIMIKRI, 24
MINI GOLF, 37
MISSING LINKS, 158
MISSION IMPOSSIBLE, 125
MISSISSIPPI, 40
MISTER MAGOO VISITS THE ZOO GAME, 169
MOD SQUAD, THE, 47
MONAD, 24
MONDAY NIGHT FOOTBALL, 27
MONEY, 98
MONKEY AUTO RACES, 48
MONKEY SHINES, 76
MONKEY'S UNCLE, 76
MONOPOLY, 56, 57
MONSTER GAME, BORIS KARLOFF'S, 144
MONSTER LAB, 67
MONSTROUS MONSTER GAME, 67
MOON FLIGHT, 69
MOSQUITO, 78
MOTHER GOOSE, A VISIT TO, 99
MOTHER'S HELPER, 87
MOUNTAIN CLIMB, 90

MOUSE CAT SCRAMBLE, 70
MOVIE GAME, THE, 111
MOVIE MOGULS, 110
MOVIE STUDIO MOGUL, 110
MOVIE TRIVIA GAME, 60
MR. BRAIN, 121
MR. DOODLE'S DOG, 91
MR. MAD, 74
MR. MAGOO GAME, THE, 169
MR. REE!, 88
MR. REMBRANDT, 74
MUSHMOUSE AND PUNKIN' PUSS GAME, 170
MUSINGO, 83
MYSTERY ZODIAC, THE, 48
MYSTIQUE FORTELL CARDS, 117

NATIONAL ENQUIRER GAME!, 141
NEO-CHESS, 24
NEVADA, 60
NEVADA 15, 60
NEVADA BLACK JACK, 60
NFL GAME PLAN, 28
NIBBLES N' BITES, 53
NO TIME FOR SERGEANTS, 16
NOAH'S ARK, 91
NOTCH, 41
NUCLEAR WAR, 16
NUMBERS UP, 64
NUTS TO YOU, 86
NUTTSY TENNIS, 31

OCTRIX, 24
OFF COURSE, 37
OFF TO SCHOOL, OFF TO CAMP, 87
OFFICIAL FOOTBALL CHESS, 26
OFFICIAL RADIO BASEBALL, 28
OH HELL, 59
OH MAGOO YOU'VE DONE IT AGAIN!, 169
OLD MAID (GIANT WHEEL), 40
OLD MAID, 58
OLD MOTHER HUBBARD, 106
OLDIES BUT GOODIES, 118
OLYMPIAD, 32
ONE MORE TIME, 95
OPEN SESAME, 76
ORBIT, 68
OUIJA, 117
OUR DEFENDERS, 12
OUR GANG TIPPLE-TOPPLE GAME, 151
OUTLAW TRAIL, 22
OVER THE GARDEN WALL, 112
OVER THE RAINBOW, 114

PAN AMERICAN WORLD JET FLIGHT GAME, 141
PANIC!, THE GAME OF, 82
PARCHEESI, 66
PAYDAY, 20
PECK'S BAD BOY WITH THE CIRCUS GAME, 148
PEGITY, 100
PERCEPTION, 115
PETER PAN, WALT DISNEY'S, 153
PETER POTAMUS GAME, THE, 171
PICTURE THIS GAME, THE, 155
PIE FACE, 89
PIGSKIN, 25
PINHEAD, 43
PINK ELEPHANT, 107
PINKY LEE AND THE RUNAWAY FRANKFURT-ERS, 163
PINKY LEE GAME TIME, 164
PIRATES OF THE BARBARY COAST, 14
PITCH-A-ROO, 81
PIVOT, 90
PIVOT POOL, 145
PIZZA PIE, 93
PLAY ON WORDS, 63
PLAY SAFE, 96
PLAY USA, 101
PLAZA, 59
PLUG-A-JUG, 79
PLUNDER, 15
POLE POSITION, 131
POLICE STATE, 118
POLICE SURGEON, 127
POLICEMAN, 98
POLLYANNA, 110
POLLYANNA DIXIE, 110
PONGO, 109
POPEYE'S 3 GAME SET, 131
POST OFFICE, 82
POT O' GOLD, 162
POW, 10
POWER 4 CAR RACING GAME, 33